P9-CZV-355

Presented to

_____

By

_____

On the Occasion of

_____

Date

_____

Finding Simplicity, Order & Insight
in a Complicated World

ANOTHER FINE MESS, LORD!

Karon Phillips Goodman

BARBOUR
PUBLISHING

ISBN 1-59789-417-6

Cover design by Mullerhaus Publishing
Cover illustration by Bryan Cooper

Published by Barbour Publishing, Inc., P.O. Box 719, Uhrichsville, Ohio 44683, www.barbourbooks.com

Our mission is to publish and distribute inspirational products offering exceptional value and biblical encouragement to the masses.

Member of the
Evangelical Christian
Publishers Association

Printed in the United States of America.
5 4 3 2 1

Contents

For my grandmothers

Introduction

Trust in the LORD with all your heart,
And lean not on your own understanding;
In all your ways acknowledge Him,
And He shall direct your paths.

PROVERBS 3:5–6 NKJV

Have enough order and peace in your life? Free of distractions and confusion? On your way to making more of your dreams come true? No? Don't worry, you're about to have all that and more, if you choose, because it's *already here*, under the mess. God has planned a great and wonderful life for you!

It's one of abundance, joy, and victory, uncluttered and unquestioned. And that's the focus of this book—*more of God* in your heart and home, more of His influence, and more attention to His presence. He didn't hide the simplicity, order, and insight you want, even under twenty years of photos and grudges or behind the clothes and habits three sizes too old. There's a special allotment just for *you*, waiting to be uncovered.

Finding it all underneath your everyday complications will be one of your greatest discoveries, even better than finding a spare car key or a stamp for your overdue house payment. We live in this world that both excites and overwhelms us—and sometimes robs us of the peace we need as much as air. We have much to do, and the demands we face quickly overpower us. That's when we drop one or two of the chain saws we've been juggling, and we cry out in pain as something bangs on the floor and maybe breaks. We close our eyes away from the chaos and cringe at the thought of having to recover and pick it all back up again.

We wonder in desperation why life is so complicated, why we can't get things together, what we're supposed to do. We dislike the taste of those questions, but we should savor them instead. Those questions are the beginning of a flight in a sky of peace. And the answers are there to hold us up, steady our fragile wings, and direct our journey—answers we find in our relationship with our Lord.

The complicated world can't claim us if we don't allow it, if we allow God to claim us instead. We can have more simplicity, order, and insight every ordinary day because we have an extraordinary God who models them for us and teaches with His love and grace. He is prepared, and we are blessed. The Lord breathes His mighty abundance on us when we make room for it. And then all is in view, because our view is filled with God, and His peace prevails over anything we can ever do to complicate our lives. Open your heart now and let the flight begin.

Part 1

What Possesses You?

If we live in the Spirit,
let us also walk in the Spirit.

<small>GALATIANS</small> 5:25 NKJV

Chapter 1

Hidden or Not?

"You sure can make a mess of things, can't you?" the Lord asked.

"You noticed, huh?"

"It's kinda hard to miss. What's the trouble?"

"Well, look at this complicated life I have! Any suggestions?"

"Lose it," He said.

"Uh, I'd love to. I could do without the mess and stress, but I need the long version of that answer, please."

"Lose it and find something else. It's *more* you need in your life if you want to have *less*."

And He calls *me* complicated?

"Trust Me on this. I will help you find everything you need for the life you want, for the life I have planned for you. Start with Me. You are Mine."

Okay, that part sounded pretty simple. Start with God. I'm game.

Do you look at day planners with their five thousand lines per page and get bleary-eyed? I do, despite the control and peace they promise. It's as if I should be able to fill every line with something profound and then, heaven forbid, should I forget any of it. The trusty notebook thicker than my dictionary may promise to streamline and organize my life, but mostly it just intimidates me. And I'm afraid to get within a hundred miles of one of those electronic calendars. With my computer (dis)abilities, I'd black out the West Coast.

Logistics and technology aren't second nature to me, but like all good, overly involved, micromanaging, obsessive maniacs, I'd fallen prey for years to the "urgency of the details" of my life. I didn't get control or peace, though. I got migraines and a sick stomach. I was possessed by the cultural mission: *Achieve! Conquer! Excel!* (and never be late, behind, or off course). It wasn't a life—it was a perpetual final exam in quantum physics: "Your mission, should you choose to accept, is to do everything in the world, be everything to the world, all at once, all by yourself. Describe the steps, and neatness counts."

Gladly. *Step 1:* Drive myself crazy. *Step 2:* Repeat Step 1.

Clearly, I would have flunked the test. But guess what? The Master Teacher intervened and let me start with Him.

"What are you looking for?" He asked me.

"Peace," I whimpered, tired and bent from the search.

"Would a simpler life bring you peace? Do you want a

little more order to your world? Is insight for all your decisions what you need?"

How'd He get so smart?

"Yep, that would do it. Know where I can find all that?"

He laughed. "It'll find *you*."

Now, that was helpful. You mean, it isn't within the pages of my calendar, not deduced from a calculus-like logic? I've been going about this all *wrong*?

"And how, pray tell, in my complicated life will it all find *me*?" I asked.

"It's *already here*, and having it is your choice. The world will always be complicated, but your life doesn't have to be. It all depends on *what possesses you*. Would you like Me to explain?"

Now it was my turn to laugh. "Uh, yes, I'm going to need the whole recipe here. Let me kick some of this clutter out of the way, and we'll get started, if You dare."

He came closer. "Not to worry. The peace you want— *My peace*—is already living inside you. Let Me wrap you in it and tell you everything."

· · · · ·

What are the biggest messes and stresses in your life right now?

_____

_____

_____

_____

Another Fine Mess, Lord!

How have you failed to sense God's peace so far?

_____

_____

_____

_____

*Lord, please give me a glimpse of Your peace today
and help me breathe the complicated world away.*

Chapter 2

Possessing or Possessed?

My mom asked what I wanted for my birthday one year. I said a dump truck, please. A rental will be fine.

"Just back it up under an upstairs window," I only half joked. "I'll have it full in about an hour."

When you can't get the door open to your storage room (and who needs a storage room anyway—doesn't that just invite your junk to stay?), you've forgotten the floor color of your bedroom, and your closet looks like a giant blender attacked it, maybe you'll want a dump truck, too. We clutter and confuse our lives far too much by all we "possess," and then we complain about it. There has to be a better way, some answer to the chaotic madness of "garbage in, garbage never out" of our lives. There has to be a simpler approach to everything out of control, a promise of peace somewhere in the piles.

"Lose it," the Lord had said about my complicated life. Maybe He meant the collection of sippy cups my college-age son could probably do without, but I believe He had something less tangible and far more important in mind. And it's that unseen clutter that fights back the hardest. That's where we need to begin, though, and just like He promised, the answers are already here.

And He said to them,
"Take heed and beware of covetousness, for one's life does not consist in the abundance of the things he possesses."
LUKE 12:15 NKJV

Jesus often spoke of the eternal unimportance of things belonging to us, of riches and possessions that promise to fulfill but only fail to bring the peace we want. Sometimes the more things we hold (that we once thought important), the less peace we have (which we once thought we could manufacture). Losing those things we don't need is certainly part of the simpler life of the tangible, but we can't stop there, or we'll miss the beautiful assurances tucked in His instructions. We don't have to limit Jesus' wisdom to material things.

UNSEEN POSSESSIONS A life filled with jealousy or bitterness or doubt or greed can't be simple, full of order or insight. It's too complicated. And a core of covetousness takes up too much space in our hearts. It squeezes out the peace God put there and then makes us wonder where it went. The culture of our time seems to demand we get more and more of everything this physical world offers, and if I can do better than you, extra points for me. We are weak and buy in to the hamster wheel of stuff and things. And we are trapped. We have no peace. We look for help.

And in that self-imposed state of confusion, we go to Jesus and get the corollary for His command. He tells us plainly that the tangible things of this life aren't what "life" is made of. Okay, but if our lives don't consist of the things we possess, then what do they consist of?

And the splendid answer comes: Our lives consist of *what possesses us*.

We are what we make room for in our hearts. We are full of peace that has lived there since we were born, if we'll just let it breathe. We can have a life of simplicity, order, and insight when we allow ourselves to be possessed by the love of God, the intangible, unsurpassed, grace-filled love of God. It's *what possesses us* that counts. That's the *more* we need in our lives if we are to have less—*more* God, *more* peace, less of everything else.

If you feel possessed by your hurting heart and engulfed by your emotional dust bunnies, you can make a different choice. It's up to you. God made His choice when time began to create a life of peace and abundance for you. When you choose more of God, the peace of a life of simplicity, order, and insight *finds you* because you've chosen to let everything contrary to it go, to "throw off everything that hinders and the sin that so easily entangles" (Hebrews 12:1 NIV).

• • • • •

"Are you getting this? Do you understand I'm not hiding anything? You don't have to live in a mess," the Lord says.

"I'm trying. But my life is like running around barefoot in the dark in a burning room full of mousetraps. I'm putting out fires and throwing ointment at wounds I can't even take the time to see. Can You fix this complicated mess, do something about this pace?"

"Yes, but that's not the same thing. Let's understand the difference, okay?"

"Okay, but make it simple, remember."

"For you, dear one, always."

. . . . .

What are you possessing today? Whatever it is, you can reject it if you want. Make a list of your "negative possessions" below. Perhaps you'll list pride or anger or laziness or procrastination or doubt. This exercise isn't meant to be brutal, but revealing. You choose everything you possess.

_____

_____

_____

Now, make a list of the "positive possessors" in your life. This list will include your love for your family, your relationship with God, your progress on your path to fulfilling your life's dream. Our plan is to be possessed by more positive forces and to possess fewer negative ones. You can *choose*. God's already made His choice—always, for you to come closer to Him, to give Him more of your life, your heart, and your home. We'll work through these choices throughout the book. This is only the beginning.

_____

_____

_____

Lord, please possess me and help me never to doubt Your presence in all the messes I make.

Chapter 3

Complicated or Busy?

Do you have a lot to do today?

Do you keep a running list next to your bed of things you want to remember?

Do you feel pressured and stressed by circumstances or memories?

Do you have obligations that don't fulfill or strengthen your relationship with God or others?

If you answered yes to the first two questions, your life is busy. If you answered yes to the last two questions, your life is complicated. There *is* a difference. And God has said it's a crystal clear choice for us to make.

"Complicated is without Me. Simple is with Me," the Lord said. "Busy is just what the world sees."

"More help here, please."

"Make the choice: Possess and complicate or be possessed and find peace. Let's look at someone here before you," He said.

Good, I could use an example.

No one would ever call Paul's life simple by even sandal-and-unleavened-bread standards, but after that little run-in between Jerusalem and Damascus, that's exactly what it became. Simple, and oh so busy.

When Paul allowed himself to be possessed by the Savior, he found peace and simplified his life because he allowed the greatest *change*. He had a goal, a passion and purpose he'd never had before, and the clutter and confusion in his mind and heart disappeared. Sure, the complicated world remained, even tightened around him, but his *life* became simple, filled with order and insight in every circumstance. A simple life with God doesn't mean one free of concerns and obligations. It means a life lived free with God the Keeper, in which our every action is based on pure devotion to Him.

It isn't the *action* that makes a life simple or complicated—it's the *attitude*. You can have a busy life that's actually quite simple or a complicated life full of nothing that matters. When you're behaving from an attitude of *belonging* instead of *owning*, of being *possessed* instead of *possessing*, you allow the peace in your heart to find you. The stress goes away, and the power of the living God rests on you, inside and out.

BUSY AND BLESSED Your life will be full because simple does not equal barren. Your life will be exciting because orderly does not equal dull. And you will live your life learning more and yet still needing more of God every day because insightful does not equal clairvoyant.

You still have plenty to do when your life becomes simple. You still need a list, but the chores and the challenges come without fear and dread because you meet them with confidence and calm. It's your *attitude*, not your action, that determines your level of peace. You meet the everyday world possessed by God, and you abandon the complicated life for one blessed and guided by a Savior who lives in the everydayness with you.

Mary certainly lived in a complicated world. She faced ridicule and rejection at an age of tender innocence and had to overcome prejudice and disbelief around her. She was a young mother and wife before disposable diapers and the pizza place on speed dial. We might think she lived one of the world's most complicated lives, but I don't think so. Yes, I'm sure her *days* were busy, but her *life* was simple. Mary said, "I am the Lord's servant" (Luke 1:38 NIV).

She followed God, she loved her family, and she let go of everything she didn't need to pursue what she did. She found simplicity, order, and insight amid the complications of a world not ready to welcome her or her story. Possessed by God's love, she lived a busy and blessed life in a complex time. We can do the same.

You may have a schedule that rivals the CEO's of any corporation, or you may have few responsibilities. It doesn't matter. How complicated or simple your life is depends not on your busyness, but your *belonging*. If you belong to God and welcome His possession of you, none of the mess in the world around you can steal your peace.

• • • • •

What is your attitude about the things that keep you busy?

_____

_____

What actions reflect your attitude? _____

_____

What actions don't? How do the complications show up in your life, in your heart, and in your home?

_____

_____

Lord, please help me simplify my attitude so that all my actions reflect Your control in my life and Your peace in my heart.
Amen.

Chapter 4

Less or More?

"These things I have spoken to you, that in Me you may have peace. In the world you will have tribulation; but be of good cheer, I have overcome the world."

I thought about this passage one day. *Sure, the world, but have You seen my calendar, my closet? Want to take a peek at my checkbook,* I challenged silently.

Know what He said?

"I am all the peace you will ever need, and I live to breathe it on you now and forever. Don't worry about all that stuff you can see. Let's start with what you can't."

Well, that sounded anything but simple. Thought I'd better clarify.

"You mean the anxiety and worry and doubt and stress and clutter in my heart? The complications I put there myself, right?"

26

"Yes, all that's far worse than the schedule and bills and dishes and laundry and everything else you're complaining about."

"Hey! I have a lot to do!" I protested.

He smiled, and His eyes twinkled like those of a toddler with a secret. "I know. And there's even more to come. I can't wait to be a part of it."

Something makes me think I'm going to want to start a new to-do list.

• • • • •

PEACE IN ABUNDANCE Before we address the clutter and chaos—that we can touch and that we can't—we need something more. Our lives aren't complicated because they're full. They're complicated because they're full of the wrong things. *More* of the God we need means *less* of everything we don't. It's so simple even I can understand.

Call it physics, call it faith, call it whatever you want. But your heart—and your home—will hold only so much. You decide what each is filled with. More of God's peace in my heart means less of my emptiness for it. More space in my home means less stuff in my way. The tangible and the intangible both adapt to the laws of science. And I can make my life and my home less complicated when I recognize how everything hinges on that choice: *more* of one thing, *less* of another. The Lord says I can start making that choice right now.

So before you prioritize your committee memberships,

color code your wardrobe, or make a trip to the city dump with the stuff from your living room floor, would you like to join me on this quest for more in our lives—more of the peace and strength and wisdom of God? It's your choice. The complicated world around you will always be there, and you can possess it if you want. Or you can be possessed by the love and power and grace of God. You can have *more of God* beginning today, ending never, if you choose. And you don't have to be any smarter or braver than you are right now. God is quite the rescuer.

LOOKING INSIDE. . .   When I told the Lord my choice for more of Him, He didn't even flinch. Considering the valley of the shadow of complications I was crawling through to get His attention, it's a wonder He didn't reconsider His offer of infinite peace. Instead, He just smiled, took my hand, and began to show me the view from His perspective, where nothing is hidden and all awaits. I have to live in the complicated, human world, but I don't have to live a complicated life. The peaceful life I want isn't something I can make—it's something I *choose* because it already exists. It doesn't come from outside me, but from *inside* me.

What do you need more of in your life? Simplicity? Order? Insight? It's all there, waiting to fill you like an underground spring, forever replenished and pure, forever able to seep into any mess and bring you peace in the everydayness of your home and work, and in the eternity of your heart and spirit. It'll find you.

Part 1

. . . . .

What do you think the Lord's view of your life is?

_____

_____

_____

_____

_____

_____

_____

_____

What do you need *more* of in your life to share His view?

_____

_____

_____

_____

_____

_____

_____

Another Fine Mess, Lord!

Lord, You know I'm even afraid to stand in a chair, but I know Your power and peace can keep me aloft, help me rise above this messy world, and soar to victories I can't even imagine. Please help me always see my life from Your view. Help me open my heart and home to all Your blessings and find the simplicity, order, and insight You've prepared just for me. I pray my spirit will reflect Yours. Please guide me in simple ways I can understand, and rest Your peace in abundance on me today. Amen.

· · · · ·

My Daily Affirmation of Peace

My life fills with more peace as I make more room
for my Lord.

Part 2

Simplicity in the Clutter

Not that I have already obtained all this, or have already been made perfect, but I press on to take hold of that for which Christ Jesus took hold of me. . . . Forgetting what is behind and straining toward what is ahead, I press on toward the goal to win the prize for which God has called me heavenward in Christ Jesus.

PHILIPPIANS 3:12–14 NIV

"Lord, please grant me a simple life."
"Beloved, I already have."

Chapter 5

Simple Is Good

He determines the number of the stars and calls them each by name. Great is our Lord and mighty in power; his understanding has no limit.

PSALM 147:4–5 NIV

I like to think the Lord adapted the KISS method for me and primed it with His loving grace: *Keep It Simple, Sweet Daughter of Mine*. He chose to let it reflect His kindness, not focus on my failures. He's seen me make a mess of just about everything at one time or another.

"You could have a simpler life, you know," He'd say.

"Oh, *why*, when I can grow complications like weeds to choke the peace out of me instead?"

Like a runaway bull in a china shop, I've wrecked the Lord's plans and upset His agenda time and again. And while the simplest way to keep the china shop intact is to bar the door to the bull, the Lord doesn't keep me away from everything breakable. Instead, He chooses to tame me and lead me through a difficult walk, through everything complicated and dangerous, with simple choices I can make every day. He lets me in and risks the messes I can make. He waits for the understanding of a daughter who wants to be less of a runaway bull.

"Could You help me with this life, Lord? I want to live it for You, but everything else keeps getting in the way. Then I can't find You because of all the clutter."

"You're looking in the wrong place. I'm in the middle of the clutter. I'm in the middle of the mess. Look for Me there, and we'll get through it together."

"Got any hip waders?"

"Several pair I've saved just for you."

I didn't know whether to be insulted or grateful. But there was no time to debate, because God was ready to meet me in the mess. He's very brave. And after me, no complications you'll ever create can scare Him away.

· · · · ·

Is anything about your life like a trampled china shop? Is there debris and brokenness, too much damage and no clue about how to repair it all? Maybe you only have one or two splintered dishes you need to clear away, and *simple* doesn't seem like such a distant concept. Or maybe you're more like me, with a whole set or two—twelve place settings, of course—shattered wall to wall. You find yourself waist deep in years of mess and complications, and a whole herd of bulls could come through and you wouldn't even notice.

What's a little more destruction? *What does it matter when I'm this far gone? I'll never know the peace of a simple life!*

We sure can dramatize things, can't we? But we can also fix them instead of wailing about them. We can have a life simple and full of God, guaranteed. No matter what condition you're living in right now, literally and spiritually, from just a little uncomfortable to certifiably insane, you can simplify it and find peace.

"I have a plan, you know," God says. "Could you stop complicating it, please? Could you yield to My order and follow My guidance for a change?"

"I'm trying. . . . My world is overwhelming. I feel inadequate."

"Nonsense. Your world is *Me*, because you are Mine, remember? I'm right here. Look at Me, know My peace, follow Me. It's not complicated."

"Okay. . .we'll see."

He just sighs at my skepticism, knowing my bullish need to be right. "Yes, we will."

Hmm, peace and simplicity for *me*? Could it be? He says yes.

· · · · ·

THE THRILL OF THE CHASE I'll tell you a little secret. Come closer. God is more excited about your quest for a simpler life than you are. Know why? It's because it will bring you closer still to Him, because there is nothing less complicated than God. *"I love you. Beginning. End. Work with Me from here. That's it."* He can be very to the point when He needs to be.

Feeling fatigued about your search for simplicity? Don't. The thrill of the chase to find and touch God's love and peace and instill His simplicity into your heart is a quest like no other, and you'll want to enjoy every second. Don't rush or worry about having to restructure hearth and home to make it happen. Don't equate *simplifying* your life with *emptying* your life. Remember, it's *more* before *less*.

Sure we want to throw away the broken dishes and outgrown obligations and all the other clutter we see and the clutter we don't, and we will. But it's what we *add* to our lives that will make all the difference. And it's not a scary or unsure task, this effort to find a simpler life, because it's not hidden or lost under a mess. It's even diagrammed for us by God Himself, filled with peace and abundance no matter how complicated the world around us gets.

Well, His life is simple because He's in charge, you point out.

I know. And your life is simple because He's in charge. You're just on a journey to see how many miraculous ways He'll show you.

· · · · ·

ALMOST TIME. . . Before we get started on our plan for a simpler life, find a pen and make some notes. Only you know how desperate your heart is for God's peace, how complicated your life is. Only you know how far you are from where you want to be. It's okay if it's a country mile or two. I'm walking it myself, and so can you.

Complete this sentence: I want to simplify my life because

_____

_____

_____

There's no wrong answer, and maybe even no complete answer, because we're growing and changing all the time. But your answer will point out to you where you're hurting the most, what you fear, what clutters your heart, and where you want to go. Now we can begin. Pray with me.

Lord, I pray for a life of more of You and less of everything in the way between You and me. I pray for Your simple touch on my heart, Your guiding hands on mine. Walk this journey with me, love me with Your forever love, and help me find the beautiful, simple life You've planned with my name on it, wrapped in Your peace. Amen.

• • • • •

Let's begin our four-part plan to finding simplicity in the clutter of our lives. Each point works in your heart and in your home. And the Lord will hold you close through every step. Simple is good.

1. Know the Truth, Tell the Truth
2. Take Responsibility for Your Choices
3. Learn from Your Mistakes
4. Have a Goal

Chapter 6

Know the Truth, Tell the Truth

Teach me your way, O LORD, and I will walk in your truth;
give me an undivided heart, that I may fear your name.

PSALM 86:11 NIV

If you and I ever meet, you might want to bring along an interpreter. I've traveled little in my life and perhaps have become a bit too comfortable with my Southern drawl. I know Miss Ruby at my local print shop understands that "ma'am" is a three-syllable word for me, but I didn't realize how likely others would be to have trouble.

My husband and I visited the Grand Canyon not long ago. Of course, it's spectacular and worth the "saddle sores" of thirty-five hundred miles, and everyone there and along the way was wonderful. But sooner or later, I'd have to open my mouth. Then they'd look at me with eyes that said, "I know she *looks* like she's from this planet, but what *is* that language she's speaking?" They'd stop all activity, focusing their stares on my face like someone trying to understand a doctor explaining a rare medical condition.

I'd repeat myself and use visual aids, like point to a map or a picture on a menu, and try to slow my speech even more. After the third or so try, they'd catch enough words to get the idea, answer quickly, and draw one of those "Wow, unbelievable!" breaths. Still, they were nice.

I think sometimes God feels like I did on my trip. He knows He's using words we should understand. He's fairly sure we're awake, He's made things as simple as possible, and yet we stand there going, "Huh?" Our misunderstanding, though, is more one of disbelief than language patterns. *Can He really be telling me the truth when He says He'll be with me always? Can my life with Him really have the peace and simplicity He promises?*

We hear His words, but we complicate the message. Sometimes we're almost a little suspicious of His absolute love. Maybe He's speaking another planet's language, and "I forgive you" really means "Gotcha!" Maybe "You are Mine" is really code for "Mess up again, and I'm done with you." But no, His love is simple and at the birth of all peace. Unlike an accent we squint our ears to understand, God's Word is simple and clear and unchanging, because His *attitude* matches His *actions*. And we can follow His example.

> *God is not a man, that he should lie,*
> *nor a son of man,*
> *that he should change his mind.*
> *Does he speak and then not act?*
> *Does he promise and not fulfill?*
>
> NUMBERS 23:19 NIV

FAILING GEOMETRY Well, I didn't technically *fail* high school geometry, but I was blamed (unjustly so) for creating the teacher's need for medication. Having to prove that two twos equal four seemed like an inane waste of my time that could be far better spent with my best friend making jewelry from clover or working on our tans. But to my poor teacher's credit, I did learn one concept that semester when she nearly retired well before her time. I learned about *congruency*—if an equation is true, it must be congruent. It must match on both sides of the equal sign. Just like God.

God said He'd send the rain, and He did. He said He'd send a sign when it was over, and He did. Noah believed, and He was saved. God was the same on both sides of the flood then, and He's the same on both sides of the "floods" we face today. If He says He will guide you, He will. If He says He will forgive you, He will.

The moving target isn't God's truth but our belief. God's example is one that will not fade, and from Him we learn the simplicity of truth, the peace of consistency. We will have it, too, when our emotions match our words, when we live a life on the outside congruent with the life on the inside. We can know the peace of congruency inspired by God's own habit.

WHY IT'S SO SIMPLE FOR HIM "Peace starts on the inside, not the outside, you know," the Lord said.

"It's not the absence of that washing machine rattle or red ink on my bank statement?"

He shook His head at me.

"Sorry, no. Peace is the absence of clutter between your heart and your hands, the simplicity of an honest life with a clear focus."

"Make it simple, please."

"It can't get any simpler—congruency equals peace," He said.

Okay, here we go.

· · · · ·

THE SIMPLE LIFE OF PAUL We've talked a little bit about Paul already. His life became simple when he began living it for the Lord. It didn't become easy, and it didn't become painless, but that's not the goal. Simplicity isn't about having nothing to do. It's about doing what we do guided by the inner peace of God. And I doubt we could find too many followers more guided by God than Paul. His life had a simplicity we can have for our own when we let the Lord possess us. We can face persecutors and doubters, meet resistance and hardship, but we keep things simple when we, too, allow our *attitude* to match our *actions*.

The entirety of Your word is truth, and every one of Your righteous judgments endures forever.
PSALM 119:160 NKJV

We complicate our lives with others when we fail to live the truth in association with them. We threaten the peace within our hearts when we fail to tell the truth to ourselves. And we jeopardize all the wonder God has breathed into our lives when we fail to understand the truth about Him. God doesn't want us to suffer through either situation, and He shows us a better, far simpler way. He tells us the truth, and then better than that, He lives it every day. There is no clutter between His heart and hands. He promises manna, and it falls. He foretells a Savior, and He is born. He offers us grace, and we receive. He will not change.

It is the habit of the Lord to tell us the truth, and we can trust Him to never waver. It is a simple relationship He's chosen with His children. His truth in our hearts will not change no matter how big a mess we make in our lives. He lives by His word, and simplicity follows.

> *For Your mercy is great above the heavens,*
> *and Your truth reaches to the clouds.*
>
> PSALM 108:4 NKJV

SIMPLE GRACE When Paul was "still breathing out murderous threats against the Lord's disciples" (Acts 9:1 NIV), he clearly lived a complicated life void of peace. He spent his time searching for followers of Christ so he could imprison them. But his misdirected life was not to last. The Lord had better plans. Unexpected, yet divinely chosen and prepared, Paul met Jesus on that dusty road and learned the core of his life forevermore.

He learned a simplicity no prison could contain. Jesus used His Father's truth as a guide when He spoke to Paul, matching His words to His actions. He simplified a man's life and a people's faith with one choice and one command.

"I am Jesus. . .get up and go into the city, and you will be told what you must do" (Acts 9:5–6 NIV). Jesus spoke the truth, and Paul chose to live it out in his life. Paul felt the congruency between his heart and his hands, even when the world around him was fractured and faithless. His simple life began with God's grace and his choice.

Christ wasted no time in getting Paul on his way to his calling. The Lord's grace had fulfilled its promise, and Jesus' focus was on the future, on the simple truth all needed to know, the truth of salvation through Him alone. Quickly, Paul was doubted by those around him and mistrusted by the disciples. We would probably have the same reaction to someone who made such a radical change. He was thought to be mad, and his life was in danger, but Paul remained true to his choice to accept the Lord's grace and follow His command. That was probably the most uncomplicated thing he ever did. And it prepared the way for the peace of God into his heart, even with chains around his body.

Before King Agrippa II, Paul recounted the walk that changed his life, telling the king without fear about his mission. Paul made it simple for all to understand, explaining how Jesus chose him to speak to the Gentiles, "to open their eyes and turn them from darkness to light, and from the power of Satan to God, so that they may receive forgiveness of sins and a place among those who are sanctified by faith in me" (Acts 26:18 NIV).

And Paul lived his life in word and deed to reflect that truth. He learned the truth of God in his heart and never doubted it, and he never failed to let it guide him in his interaction with others. He made things simple by building on what he knew to be true and settling for nothing less from himself. The *actions* of his hands matched the *attitude* of his heart. Paul made his choice and simplified his life. We can do the same.

THE TRUTH OF GOD

The mind controlled by the Spirit is life and peace.
ROMANS 8:6 NIV

We simplify our lives when we base them first on God's truth to us, on His meeting us on our messy road where we must make a choice, just like Paul. When we know Him intimately and believe in His personal touch, we see His dominion over our lives, which we can change for the better.

The truth of God's grace is that He saves us from ourselves, over and over. He takes away the clutter if we'll let Him and replaces it with peace. He makes the complicated simple when we rest in His truth, trusting that He will not lie or deceive us, give us any job we can't handle, or withhold any blessing we need.

O LORD, You are my God. I will exalt You,
I will praise Your name, for You have done wonderful things;
Your counsels of old are faithfulness and truth.
ISAIAH 25:1 NKJV

Trusting in His infinite care and concern for us means believing He is who He says He is. That one choice will simplify our lives with a foundation no earthly mess can hide. It's the lack of belief in our salvation that complicates our lives. Simplicity starts from within, every time, no matter how full your to-do list is. If your days are a mess, it's because your heart is a mess.

EVERY DAY IS TODAY We sort of *know* there must be a way to escape the infinite quandary that just keeps getting stronger and stronger, some way to remove the spiritual clutter taking our breath away. But who has the time or courage to look? The complicated world of family, work, and responsibilities demands answers and decisions, choices and changes. But we can't simplify the *everyday* part of our lives and meet the tangible demands of where to go and what to do until we simplify the *eternal* part of our lives.

Can you trust God's forgiveness and love? Are you living through His grace, or do you think it's not meant for you? Do you imprison yourself, complicate your life with doubts, because you won't allow yourself to believe and hold the peace of God?

Often our lives get complicated because we fail to see how precious we are in God's eyes. Without that foundation, we can't go forward on any kind of peaceful flight. Without the trust in His words to accept us regardless of our flaws and to welcome us because of His love, nothing is simple. We are always fighting for that invaluable sense of belonging, making "murderous threats" to everything we don't understand, and walking on the eggshells of a soul who knows no faith. But we can have something more when we know what we need first.

"Seek first the kingdom of God and His righteousness, and all these things shall be added to you" (Matthew 6:33 NKJV). Simplify your quest, He says. Believe in God's care and undying presence, and save yourself the complications of a life of doubt.

When you believe you are His treasured child, you please God with your trust. And He delights in the opportunity to prove it to you. Seek His kingdom with the excitement and expectation of a loved child, and hold on to everything you find. You can simplify your choices amid all kinds of opposition or distraction. Abraham knew how to do that in the greatest test of all. "You see that his faith and his actions were working together, and his faith was made complete by what he did" (James 2:22 NIV).

Ask God to be close to you and feel Him completely consume you. Ask Him to forgive you and feel Him completely renew you. Ask Him to speak to you and feel Him completely guide you. He'll do nothing in a small way. God made you special and whole. Like the love of a parent for a child, there was nothing simpler and more direct than God's actions when He breathed you to life. And His attitude about you hasn't changed. Learn that, and you simplify every mess you could ever bring into your life.

• • • • •

THE TRUTH WE LEARN ABOUT OURSELVES Jesus called Paul "a chosen vessel of Mine" (Acts 9:15 NKJV), and I have no doubt He calls you and me the same. No, we don't have Paul's mission, but we have a mission unique and necessary just the same. Do you feel the Lord leading you on your mission today? Are you where you want to be in your life? Are you confident and secure in your work for Him? If you are, then you know the simplicity this guarantees. And if not, you will discover it.

Sometimes we can be like Moses or Jonah and fight God's instructions at first. Maybe we feel inadequate or we're afraid. But we don't have to when we remember God created us with a purpose to fulfill in this lifetime. Everybody else may be scattered and confused, lost or over-whelmed by the volume of life around them. But you can walk calmly and in peace through every storm when you know you're honoring the great truth God placed inside you. No matter where you live or what kind of tangible life you lead, you simplify the mess and quiet the noise when you don't deny your purpose.

We do like to give the Lord a challenge now and then, though, and go against the simple plan He's devised. I'm sure you know the results. It's sort of like when I try to cook. After a few close calls with the stomach pump, I'm comfortable with the truth: I can't do it. I've made things the dog wouldn't even eat.

You may know the lack of peace associated with something far more important than my cooking, and you always have a choice about how to make it better. Maybe you're trying to excel in a career you didn't choose. Maybe you're trying to be a kind of person you don't feel comfortable being. Admit what doesn't fit, then grant yourself permission to pursue the truth your heart is crying out to live, to be the person God birthed you to be. Don't be scared. (We'll talk more about this great part of our walk with God in Part 4 of our book.)

ONLY YOU God made us all different and yet loves us all the same. We complicate His plan when we try to live a life other than our own. Maybe you think you're simplifying things by sticking with the status quo, by not daring to dream, but the opposite happens. Simple is only simple when it makes sense, and it makes sense to follow God's lead.

> *The LORD will fulfill his purpose for me;*
> *your love, O LORD, endures forever—*
> *do not abandon the works of your hands.*
>
> PSALM 138:8 NIV

It's the same point of congruency again. Until we feel God's peace between our hearts and our hands, everything will be complicated, and it will be of our own choosing. God's peace is found in His love for us and in how we live out our lives for Him. Knowing and choosing the simple route is choosing to be the disciple He created you to be. I'm one who can't cook, and that's okay.

Don't let a complicated mess discourage you. It seems we all have to taste the lack of truth before we can savor its flavor when we claim it for ourselves. Once you get just an inkling of what it's like to live in the truth about yourself, you'll never want anything else. You'll feel the amazing clarity and focus and blessed simplicity it brings to your life. There will be no clutter to complicate things, because clutter is always there where truth isn't. It's like dust collected on a priceless antique. The piece doesn't change, but it's masked in what doesn't belong. Rid yourself of the grime of spiritual clutter and reveal your truth starting today.

Every mess you go through turns you into the disciple you are becoming. Every time you fall, get back up again, and turn to God for His truth, simplicity follows and you grow. That strong and capable disciple is who you truly are!

I imagine Paul felt anything but capable to meet the truth God told him, considering his previous job description. But God knew better. He gave Paul a job to do and the ability to do it. He prepared for him a place and a passion that matched Paul's qualifications. Don't you want the same kind of joy from your journey Paul had? It will *find you* when you embrace the honesty in your heart.

$$\bullet \quad \bullet \quad \bullet \quad \bullet \quad \bullet$$

THE TRUTH WE TELL OTHERS

Do not lie to each other, since you have taken off your old self
with its practices and have put on the new self,
which is being renewed in knowledge in the image of its Creator.

COLOSSIANS 3:9–10 NIV

"Want to simplify things some more?" God asks.

"Sure, I do!"

"Don't hide your truth from others, okay?"

"Okay, how?" I need to know.

"Live every day as the new person I'm growing you to be. That's all."

All? Sounds like a lot. What does growing have to do with honesty and simplicity? Let's see. . . . If I'm following God's truth and learning to honor the truth about myself, I have to be changing, first on the inside and then for everyone else to see. If I want the simplicity I've created in my heart to become part of my home and my life, the honesty has to continue. If it doesn't, I can't grow anymore; I can't become the more valuable disciple I want to be.

Do not let any unwholesome talk come out of your mouths,
but only what is helpful for building others up
according to their needs,
that it may benefit those who listen.

EPHESIANS 4:29 NIV

We rarely set out to live an untruth, but when we do, the complications rain on us without end. We get ourselves in all kinds of uncomfortable situations because we feel one thing in our hearts and display something else to the world. That lack of congruency takes away any peace we can hope for. It's the same as denying a truth to ourselves, except that we involve others and bring in even more clutter. And the by-products of dishonesty (depression, guilt, shame, anxiety, loss of respect) grow faster than you can contain them. Nothing is simple because you've lost sight of the example you're following: God.

The Lord's truth of unending love and care gives us the strength to carry on in our complicated world. His devotion that never changes makes us able to withstand all the changes of a time that moves fast and furiously. We simplify things when we remember to hold on to the Lord's truth, honor the truth He's taught us about ourselves, and reflect that truth to others. Then the peace we need finds us.

LIVING THE TRUTH I've found a simple prayer that helps me stay on track to the place of peace and avoid cluttering up my life with lies or deceit. I copied it from David:

> *Let the words of my mouth*
> *and the meditation of my heart*
> *be acceptable in Your sight, O LORD,*
> *my strength and my Redeemer.*
>
> PSALM 19:14 NKJV

David asks that what he says *and* what he thinks be acceptable to God. I think that's the key. *Put me in Your will,* he's asking God.

I try to remember to say that prayer every morning before I get out of bed. It reminds me to trust God's promise to tell me the truth, to guide me in His ways, and to go with me on this great journey. I pray for more of God to come into my heart so that I know His great plans and purposes for me. I pray for the courage to overcome the harmful leanings of my human spirit and instill the grace I've learned from God in their place. I pray for the wisdom to reflect to others the truth I trust, to find the peace honesty promotes.

Telling your truth may mean refusing to participate in a friend's gossip fest anymore. It may mean bowing out of a cause you don't believe in but your family or friends support. It may mean living a life of quiet and frugality when your friends live otherwise. Any of these examples may look like the complicated choice, but it's actually the one that will give you peace because your *attitude* will match your *actions*. We can simplify our lives now, or we can live with the mess for a long time to come.

A couple of common issues we complicate in our lives are money and position. If we live a lifestyle we can't afford on the outside just to impress someone or "fit in," we're going to have to live with the consequences. If we profess to be something we're not or claim achievements we haven't met, we're going to have to live with the consequences. And peace and simplicity are not among them. When you make the choice to live those kinds of lies, you bring destructive clutter into your heart. Like steel stakes driving into the ground, those choices keep you mired in anxiety and unhappiness, and there's no way to take flight with God's great purpose. There's no real you showing, and all the grand experiences of your *true* life are lost. Your heart aches, and the Lord grieves right along with you.

The truth of your life now and the wonder of what it will become are too great to waste in dishonesty. The only simple life is one that lives the congruency between your heart and your hands, between what you know and what you do. That doesn't mean everything is easy, but it does mean a life of peace. Just look at Paul.

• • • • •

How will you simplify your life by believing and living in God's truth?

_____

_____

_____

_____

How will you simplify your life by living your truth as God's "chosen vessel" and striving for congruency between your *attitude* and your *actions*?

_____

_____

_____

How will you simplify your life by telling your truth to others?

_____

_____

_____

Chapter 7

Take Responsibility for Your Choices

When we've already made bad choices and created all kinds of complications, we make things even worse when we victimize our situation. Simplicity is about a clear view of all we touch, physically and spiritually, about knowing and living the truth. If we blame others for complicating our lives with their choices, we forget the power of our own. Paul understood about choices, and he knew how to simplify the results, too.

Christ Jesus came into the world to save sinners—
of whom I am the worst. But for that very reason I was
shown mercy so that in me, the worst of sinners, Christ Jesus
might display his unlimited patience as an example for those
who would believe on him and receive eternal life.

1 Timothy 1:15–16 NIV

Paul took responsibility for his choices and then claimed the grace of God. How's that for keeping it simple?

Sure, Paul could have blamed any number of people or policies for his actions, but he didn't. And if we look around, we can always find someone else to hold accountable or some situation to blame for creating the mess in our lives. The truth, though, is always found with *us*. Facing it allows us to deal with it, and then we can go on to more wonderful choices, because God is standing there ready to help us find peace in every circumstance.

FINALLY READY We probably won't find ourselves inside the belly of a fish anytime soon, but we can relate to Jonah's choice to flee "from the presence of the LORD" (Jonah 1:3 NKJV). We've done the same thing many times. And finally, when we're face-to-face with our situation, we can deny our involvement or prepare for something better. Jonah took responsibility for his actions and was answered by the Lord.

> *"I went down to the moorings of the mountains;*
> *The earth with its bars closed behind me forever;*
> *Yet You have brought up my life from the pit, O LORD, my God."*
> JONAH 2:6 NKJV

Poor choices don't mean we'll never get it right. They don't banish us to the edges of God's patience or destroy the truth still inside us. He is the God of second chances, no matter how many we need. We dishonor Him when we don't give Him a chance to redeem us through our error, to guide us in our lostness. If we want to simplify things, we start where we are today, not later when things settle down. If you're like me, that "settling down" time will never come. Instead, I can choose *today* to pray, "Yes, this mess is of my own making, Lord, but I know You're bigger than any mess I could ever make. Please show me what to do with this one."

Then we reflect His words in everything we do. We can be strong enough to take responsibility for our choices and then humble enough to go to God for forgiveness. That's where the peace begins. It's never in escaping something that's ours, but in taking it and making it better. That's what God does with each of us.

The Lord is the greatest responsibility assumer *ever*. He has to deal every day with *me*, but He doesn't blame the universe or the stock market or the weather—He just says, "Yeah, she's Mine, I'll never leave her." He claims me and spends every day trying to make me better. He couldn't do that if He disowned me. And we can't make any of our choices better if we disown them.

Let's look at a few everyday times when we might be tempted to shirk our responsibilities.

- Have you unjustly accused someone of something (or maybe you have the tendency to jump to conclusions regularly)? Take responsibility for that, and apologize for anything in the past, while practicing to keep an open mind and quiet tongue in the future. Take the time to recognize and restrict the actions that bring you all kinds of complications, so you can find more peace. *That will simplify everything that follows.*

- Have you abandoned a dream while you let "life" or others take the blame? Take responsibility for that, and decide if you want to pursue your dream again. If so, know that you will be the reason it comes true or not, as you make choices that allow it or not. "Life" will always be in the way, and you decide if your dream will be a part of it. *That will simplify everything that follows.*

- Are you always struggling with a messy home, while allowing too many chores to fall on you? Take responsibility for that, and establish a few new rules, such as no food in the bedrooms or wash your own dishes or leave your shoes at the door. Eliminate the stress (and teach personal responsibility to your kids) by sharing what has been "your" job with the rest of your family in as many ways as you can. *That will simplify everything that follows.*

- Have you over obligated yourself in a friendship, a cause, your job, or your finances? Take responsibility for that, and begin clearing up any misconceptions or misunderstandings you've allowed, while you walk with God toward better uses of your time and resources. Sometimes we allow ourselves to be influenced by others, or we try something, and it fails. It happens to all of us, and complications result. Once we recognize a destructive pattern, we can reorient ourselves to obligations we are suited for and want to fulfill. *That will simplify everything that follows.*

- Have you procrastinated about decisions you need to make or accepted the way things are instead of working to change them? Take responsibility for that, and develop a plan to tackle what isn't working, starting today; or twenty years from now, everything will be the same but with twenty years of dust on top of it. Complications abound when we do nothing in a situation that calls for action. No one is responsible for your life but you, and when you choose to take control of it, the Lord intervenes to help. *That will simplify everything that follows.*

The pattern is the same no matter what situation you're trying to understand and improve. Take responsibility for your actions and enjoy the simplicity that follows. What a good plan. The opposite doesn't work very well at all.

"IT'S NOT MY FAULT!" The person with a lot of complications and clutter in her life is the person who professes a dozen times a day, about everything that happens to her: "It's not my fault!" And while much of what happens in our lives truly isn't our fault—we can't control the weather or others' choices and actions—much of what happens to us to rob us of our peace is at least an indirect result of "our" fault. Let's look at an example.

Let's say you're writing a paper for a class or a report for work. Let's say you've waited until the evening before it's due to begin. Let's say there's a power failure or your computer dies. Is that your fault? No, you can't control those things, but your paper will be late because you failed to *prepare* for the things you couldn't control by waiting until the last day to do the work. If you had begun earlier so there'd still be time after failed power or computers had been corrected, you'd still have gotten the work done on time.

Learning to anticipate these kinds of situations brings loads of simplicity to your life. The clutter in your work and in your mind is nonexistent when you take responsibility for your choices by preparing the best you can for what you can't control. "Be prepared in season and out of season" (2 Timothy 4:2 NIV).

Taking responsibility for your choices isn't about placing blame or hanging more guilt around your neck. It's just a fact that we can only affect what's ours. It's tough to have to react to those things we can't control (power and mechanical failures), but when we act on what we can (our attitude and preparation for work, anticipation of problems), then we've taken a step toward kicking all the clutter and complications out of the way. It doesn't make our lives harder to take responsibility, but calmingly simpler.

• • • • •

Where have you failed to take responsibility for your choices, and how has that complicated your life?

_____

_____

_____

_____

How will you change that, starting today?

_____

_____

_____

_____

Chapter 8

Learn from Your Mistakes

But now that you know God—or rather are known by God—
how is it that you are turning back to those
weak and miserable principles?
Do you wish to be enslaved by them all over again?
GALATIANS 4:9 NIV

*Well, I did it again. . .*we say. And the "it" can be anything.
God's response is always the same:

What did you learn?

I love to look at Paul's life and find hope for mine.
Paul probably learned more from his mistakes than any
of us ever will, and we can see the effects of his efforts.
Rarely do we have to live blind for three days to adopt this
practice into our lives.

The Lord gives us a new start every day and graciously
allows our lives to be uncluttered from the past. We don't
have to haul around the regret and pain and fear that
only complicates our days, because instead, we can learn

from it. Failures and mistakes strangle the breath of today when we hang on to them, but releasing them frees us to think and grow unencumbered. And that brings peace and simplicity.

We make *little* mistakes every day—such as locking our keys in the car—but we simplify our lives when we learn from these mistakes so we don't repeat them—when we learn to carry an extra key with us. Then there are *bigger* mistakes—saying things in a careless way that hurt a friend's feelings. We simplify our lives when we find a better and more sensitive way to have a discussion. And then there are the *biggest* mistakes—the times we fail to honor the truth about God and ourselves and make a real mess of things. The complications only get worse when we let these mistakes possess us. We can, instead, let God possess us and accept His grace and guidance. That makes things pretty simple—yes, it's a mistake, but it's a lesson, too. Fail, learn, carry on. It's a simple pattern.

"Those who are wayward in spirit will gain understanding; those who complain will accept instruction."
ISAIAH 29:24 NIV

SIMPLE LESSONS Some of the hardest, and longest-lasting, lessons we learn come in times of trial, when we've hurt others and have to live with those consequences. Overcoming those kinds of mistakes takes lots of time and more prayer. It's tough to escape the pain and move on to any kind of simplicity. We are too hurt and too ashamed to get past the complications we've brought into our lives. But it doesn't have to stay that way. God is waiting to come into our hearts and replace the pain with something else, with His wisdom and grace and understanding. He knows our failures, but He stands ready to fix us. He loves us so we can learn.

> *Yet the LORD longs to be gracious to you;*
> *he rises to show you compassion.*
> *For the LORD is a God of justice.*
> *Blessed are all who wait for him!*
>
> ISAIAH 30:18 NIV

And there's a great use for these mistakes we'd like to pretend didn't exist. Like a graduate student still learning but able to teach, you can draw on what you learn from your mistakes to help others with the same struggles. If you've overcome a painful past, you're equipped to help others do the same. You don't have to be beaten by a history that's less than perfect when you can use it somehow today. Teach me what you've learned.

Paul's life with Christ was completely opposite his life before. He had much to overcome, but he was able to accept the Lord's forgiveness and redemption and then become the person he was born to be. You can do the same when you won't settle for anything less than your unique calling, when you pursue and honor the truth about yourself and learn from your mistakes along the way.

Part 2

TESTS TO TEACH US

The crucible for silver and the furnace for gold,
but the LORD tests the heart.

PROVERBS 17:3 NIV

When silver and gold are refined at high temperatures, they become pure, free of damaging and useless substances. Our hearts do the same thing in the "trials of fire" we experience throughout our lives.

And it's a solitary fire. None of us can ever know exactly what someone else goes through, and none of us can ever hand off our tests to others. It's a personal time of struggle, but God makes sure we aren't alone. What do we do when times get tough and scary? We cry out, "Oh, my God!" And what does He do? He answers, "Yes? Here I am." The tests hurt, but they don't hide us from our Lord.

And there's something else the Lord does for us, too. He never fails to point out the effects of our fire, no matter what the cause. He tucks a lesson inside every lapse. He wastes nothing because He sees to it that we pass all His tests—not by becoming perfect or free from pain, but by refining our hearts to make them more like His. Isn't that what you feel after every trial—a renewed closeness and identity with God and a new lesson to hold in your heart? Silver and gold glisten in newfound light.

The more we learn, the less likely we'll be to repeat a mistake. In a notebook, keep a record for a while. Keep it simple, just two columns: your mistakes and the lessons you learn from each. Maybe you'll note cruel criticisms or uncaring words, lack of preparation at work or poor driving habits. Pay attention and note how complications you could avoid drip into your days. Simplify everything to come with the lessons you learn.

One fire endured is one impurity removed. And remember, it's not about the fire, but what remains and what recedes after it.

And we know that in all things
God works for the good of those who love him,
who have been called according to his purpose.

ROMANS 8:28 NIV

• • • • •

Have you tried to forget mistakes in the past instead of learning from them? What happened?

_____

_____

_____

_____

How can you begin to look at your mistakes differently and use them to simplify your life?

_____

_____

_____

_____

Chapter 9

Have a Goal

Draw near to God and He will draw near to you.
JAMES 4:8 NKJV

"I can tell you how to bring *even more* simplicity to your life if you want to know," God said.

"Of course. Any chance it will help straighten out some of these messes?"

"It's guaranteed to if you follow what I teach you."

"Right away? Please say, right away."

He paused.

Uh-oh.

"Let's not worry about the timing right now, okay? Let's just keep it simple."

He smiled at me as I peered over all the clutter I'd created.

"There's hope for this mess?"

"Your focus is off again. Look at *Me*. There's plenty of hope for all My messy children, even you."

"Okay, for *even me*, what's this way to even more simplicity?"

"More of Me in you, in your goals."

That one was going to need some explaining, too. I was having a hard time not panicking about the clock and not focusing on the mess, but we were off again.

• • • • •

We have to remember that simplifying our lives isn't about emptying them, but *filling* them instead. You want to rid yourself of the clutter of old habits and unhealthy relationships, but your pursuit of a goal for *more of God* in your heart will simplify your life best, He says. Our primary goal is to live our lives for God. If we keep our focus there, then all that follows, big and small, will coincide with that one choice. *That* makes things simple.

Sometimes we don't even realize how we complicate things by choosing goals that destroy our peace. Seeking revenge or plotting to hurt someone else will never be where God wants us to be. It's tough to hear Him when we've filled our heads and hearts with manipulation or deceit. But God keeps trying until we know we can go on no longer without His peace in our lives. He keeps reaching out to us because He is the *ultimate* goal setter.

God never loses sight of *you*. Your name is always on His lips, your heart eternally connected to His. Nothing can keep Him from you, because you're too important to Him (remember that truth that never changes?). When He has the priority of being with you on the top of His list, everything else—guiding you, forgiving you, comforting you—follows without a hitch. He stands ready to help you refocus your goals when you need to so you can carry on with your walk with Him. The work is done because He stays true to His goal, and we can follow His example. We can let our goal of being near God and responding to His call become our beacon.

GETTING CLOSER Paul knew how to follow a goal. He had one job, and he alone was qualified for it. The same is true for you. Only you know what your life is destined to become. Only you can choose for yourself how you will live it. And peace comes in keeping things simple.

When you preface every choice with this question—Will this action get me closer to my goal of living for God?—you will have a response of yes or no. Then you can apply the same reasoning to all the other goals in your life, the goals of education, career, family, and the continuing growth in your relationships. See? It's not so complicated, after all, when we start with the big goals that define who we are and work our way through the smaller ones.

If it's your goal to go back to school and earn a degree, you may have to work two jobs to pay your tuition. On the outside, that looks like a very complicated life. But in your heart, it's quite simple because you're making the choice that gets you closer to your goal. When there's congruency between your attitude (your goal) and your actions (your choice), you're living a simple life, even with all the clutter around you. And peace *finds you* because you're honoring the truth within your heart.

When you bring the joy and energy of goals into your life, everything contrary to them goes away. You fill your heart with more of God and His wisdom and direction, and you let go of anything that doesn't match. It's *more* before *less*, and the result is simplicity, no matter how long it takes.

THE GOAL CONTINUES Paul says, "It is God who works in you to will and to act according to his good purpose" (Philippians 2:13 NIV), so He's not finished yet, either. He knows the struggles we have, and He continues to work in us every moment, helping us to stay on track with our goals and overcome the human tendency we have to complicate everything. (He has lots of work to do with some of us who shall remain nameless.)

Sometimes we create the biggest complication of all by misinterpreting our goals as chores. When we see drudgery and obligation, we're not looking at the right things. Mopping the floors may be a *chore*, but creating the home you want is a goal. Apologizing may be a *chore*, but becoming more sensitive to others' feelings is a *goal*. It's critical that we understand the difference.

Chores are perhaps the "housekeeping" parts of a goal, and because we live in the real world where floors get dirty and feelings get hurt, we have to pay attention to them. But the chores are never what will drive us to grow and have the life we want. That has to come from the *inside*, from something far bigger, from a goal that holds our attention and keeps our focus on the peace it guarantees.

Every goal must be part of our passion if it's ever going to matter enough to us to work for it. Then we can make things simple. Then we see, over time and trial, mistakes and lessons, how all work that is a passion will always get done. We are still the same flawed disciples with much to learn, but we can let the peace of a goal-centered life settle on us like the warmth of summer that comes in its own time. And it's not complicated when we remember where our goals originate.

Only when we're in tune with God's plans for us can we go forward, one breath at a time, happily striving for the accomplishment of yet another goal, enjoying the journey as much as the destination. That's how you'll know if your goal matters enough to be part of your life, if you're pursuing it for the right reasons.

It's true for everything you want to call a goal, for getting your education, completing a project at work, or painting your house. Every goal can become complicated if you make it so by pursuing it for the wrong reasons, because it's expected of you or because it's trendy or convenient. Every *sincere* goal becomes simple, no matter how busy you are in reaching it, if you pursue it as part of your walk with God.

Now, what does painting my house have to do with my walk with God? you ask. I know it sounds odd, but everything we do to create change in our lives is about growing and becoming something *else*, something *more*, because we evolve along the way. You're not the same person when you pursue and complete a goal, when you're "renewed in the spirit of your mind" (Ephesians 4:23 NKJV). You're closer to God every time.

A LONG ROW TO HOE My husband and I have worked for five years to update, repair, and renovate our 120-plus-year-old house so we can sell it. I look at everything we do and everything left to do, and it's easy to get discouraged. But while things may seem complicated on the outside, it all remains quite simple. Each action comes after the answer to "Will this get us closer to our goal?" Each struggle sends me to the Lord for guidance and support, and there He teaches me.

Because this goal is so important to me, it's a big classroom, an audience at the throne of God with revelations I wouldn't receive otherwise. I've had to learn and live all those things the physical struggles teach, the perseverance, adaptability, and patience for the fruit of this long growing season. Sometimes I think it's like God's work on me—so far to go and yet He doesn't give up.

Still far from seeing the completion of this goal, my passion only deepens, despite the time and trials. For now, I have to work where I am and hold on to my goal when it's buried under other real-life messes I can't control. And yet the thought of it keeps me inspired and excited, the hope abounding in each new day I haven't given up. May God find the same hope in me.

How about you? What goal is taking forever to come to you? Does it seem too complicated to pursue? Are you considering giving up? If so, here's one way to reignite your fire for your goal or kindle it elsewhere. Only you'll know.

Consider the alternative. You can always choose *not* to pursue your goal. Think through that option and see if you start to itch and wrinkle your face all over and it hurts to breathe. That's what happens to me when I think of abandoning the work this old house needs. The effort to complete the work so we can move is harder than the choice to stay, but staying isn't simpler or more peaceful, because that alternative complicates everything that follows for my heart and soul. And *that's* what physical goals have to do with your walk with God.

Your spiritual world is eternally entwined with your physical world, because that's where we live these messy lives. We have to work within the confines of the world we know to learn more about the world we don't, the world of God. He comes to us where we are, and He helps us choose the path to carry us where He wants us to be. He uses what we can touch and affect to help us become something *more*, something *else*. He takes our loaves and fishes and ministers to us and to the world through our goals. See your physical work as something spiritual at the heart, because that's what it is. Choose your goals well, because that's where you'll meet God.

ACHIEVING THE GOAL When you do choose a right goal for yourself and meet it as you planned, you'll do a little victory dance with God. There is great reward. And then you want more, and you see the relationship between all goals and your walk with God, bending to His timing and searching His will as you strive to complete your own. You'll reach your goal of earning your degree or learning another language or opening a business, and then there will be *more*. You'll reach your goal of accepting God's grace or forgiveness or learning to trust His timing, and then there will be *more*.

Our primary goal of becoming nearer to God continues always and births for us new goals every day. We'll look at our lives a year from now and think we've simplified things in amazing ways. Then we'll look back ten years from now and see how little we had learned at that time! And that's okay. We're always learning, always discovering ways to simplify, always finding *more* of God's peace.

Everything builds on what came before it, and one success leads to others. Sure, we fail and, in the process, sometimes have to reassess our goals and make tough choices. But we don't lose our connection with God as long as we keep our heart touching His. It's as simple as that.

CHARTING YOUR PROGRESS Let's develop a worksheet to help us keep a record of our goals. At the top of a piece of paper (or on the computer, if you're more high-tech than I am), label four columns: *Attitude, Action, Adjustment, Reward*. You can add more goals or reevaluate the ones you choose today. Remember, the ultimate goal is a peaceful life with God close to you. Keep it simple, and everything else will follow.

For each goal, describe your:

- *Attitude*—What about the goal makes it important at this stage of your life? Why do you feel enough passion about this point to make it a goal? Would abandoning the goal go against everything you feel in your heart?

- *Action*—What will you do each day to get you closer to your goal? What will you do to resist the actions that won't further your goal? What will you allow into your life that helps you grow and become more of the disciple God knows you can be?

- *Adjustment*—What has changed about your heart and soul since you began work on your goal? How are you adjusting the balance of *more* and *less* in your life? How do you feel more of God and less of anything contrary to your truth?

- *Reward*—Of course, the big reward will come when you and God achieve your goal. But you'll find lots of little victories along the way to reassure you and sustain you when the messes keep piling up around you. Chart your progress and look forward with great confidence and expectation to the day you note each goal finished and delivered. Then you can do the little happy dance with God again. It's His victory, too.

Finally, think about how each of your goals falls in line with your primary goal of living for God. If you can't see where one does, investigate what you're missing, what you might have misinterpreted, or where some other great blessing may lie. God is waiting for you.

And let us not grow weary while doing good,
for in due season we shall reap if we do not lose heart.

GALATIANS 6:9 NKJV

Chapter 10

Peace in the Mess— Breathing in Your Water

When we begin to pursue a simpler life, we think it begins with the overstuffed closet and the overbooked calendar. But it doesn't. Those are not the causes but the effects of complications we've allowed into our lives because we've misunderstood so much. We've neglected or ignored the truth, we've failed to learn what our lives stand ready to teach us, and we have our priorities all mixed up. We ask our Lord for a simple life, not knowing He's already prepared it.

That life we want is one lived in the grace of God, following His lead and embracing His passion. We make things simple when we accept the life already there for us, when we see how everything relates to our basic choice of *more of God* or *more of something else*. And when we choose more of God, He opens the floor of heaven and floods our hearts with peace. He pursues us where the most threatening complications live, and He offers a simple alternative.

"Breathe in your water," He says.

It took me forty years to learn how to live this command, to understand what He meant. You can't really hold water on your skin, but you know it's there, without any pressure or pain. The water He spoke of is your life's purpose as it was meant to be—all around you, the essence of what you are, the rhythm of your soul. Your water is your calling, and it may take several forms. Because you are one person with many abilities and gifts, you have many opportunities in your life to excel, to live as God intended. And when you do, you see how simple what you've always thought was complicated turns out to be. Your clarity is brilliantly bright, stunningly accurate, always on time. I found that clarity and simplicity in my work, part of the water God made for me.

He who began a good work in you
will carry it on to completion until the day of Christ Jesus.
PHILIPPIANS 1:6 NIV

Before I understood how to breathe in my water, I was like a fish dropped on a pier. He's lost, and yet he flops continuously, drawn by something he can't quite see but knows is his only safe place. He keeps flopping, flopping, hoping he's read his instincts correctly, almost out of breath, feeling alone, forsaken, and about to give up when, with the final flop, he falls into the lake. He finds safety at last. He can't quite believe he's made it, but he relishes the right feel of the water. It's all he knows, and he realizes it's all he'll ever know. And yet it's all he needs. His life is where he is, home at last.

My work was hard when I pursued it apart from the rhythm God gave me, when I flopped on the pier. Breathing in your water starts when you allow yourself to trust your rhythm, the gentle, intuitive ebb and flow of your body, spirit, and mind. It's scary at first, but it's the only way to peace.

When I finally began to look at why my work was hard, I saw what God was trying to tell me. Living in me from the very beginning was a wisdom that said, "Trust your rhythm, your work will not suffer, you will finish." But it had frightened me, and I shoved the echo away and continued with my oppressive, uncomfortable pattern. Still, God didn't give up, and the voice became more insistent. I had to learn to listen to my body and my mind where the work of my spirit was concerned. The goals I had were suffering because I was neglecting the grandest goal of all, of bringing *more of God* into what I was trying to manage on my own.

Before I understood my water, there would be times I was so exhausted I could barely think, and yet I'd feel compelled to work anyway. My rhythm would protest and say, "No, you should rest, but you are still working. . . ." That was the part of my water I had rejected, the part that supported me even when I couldn't feel it. My work had a rhythm, too, that had adapted itself to my soul, so that even when I was stopped, I was still working, because everything I do makes its way into my work somehow. Every sentence has to run loose in my mind a while before it connects to the ones around it, and that sometimes happens best when I'm quiet and still.

When I saw the pause and rest as part of my work, I saw how simple the process was that I'd tried to complicate, how much more important the work was than the clock, just as He said. God was speaking to me and teaching me through everything I did, and when I began to relax into what He was doing with my life and this goal, I could breathe the peace He offered through every mess I made. I was breathing in the water He made for me.

• • • • •

Lord, thank You for loving me always, especially every time I make another fine mess. I know You won't stop loving me, because that's who You are, and that truth brings great simplicity to my life. Please help me simplify even more as I strive to learn from my past, honor You in my present, and achieve the goals You want for me in the future. Help me breathe in my water You've made just for me, because that's where my peace is, where You are. Thank You for simplifying my life. Amen.

• • • • •

My Daily Affirmation of Simplicity

A simple life is a life of simple choices toward the goals of my heart.

Part 3

Order in the Chaos

For God is not a God of disorder but of peace.
1 CORINTHIANS 14:33 NIV

"Lord, please bring order to my life."
"Beloved, I already have."

Chapter 11

Order When You Ask

Quick, where is everything you need, your list of everything you need to do, and your plan to take care of it all? Can you rest easy at night knowing your heart and home are in order, nothing out of place, nothing lost or forgotten? Come on. . .I need an answer. What are you waiting for?

Sorry, didn't mean to pick on you there. Maybe I was talking to myself about the chaos of *my* days, or maybe you can relate? Do your home and heart run smoothly? Are you prepared and in control of the everydayness of your life? Or do you feel as organized as a can of worms and wonder if you'll *ever* get your life together? If so, you'll be glad to know I've found a way through the chaos, a Guide to follow: our Lord, always prepared and in control. He is the Master Organizer, never caught unaware, never frustrated by His responsibilities, never behind in His work. We can have order, too, when we follow His example and learn what He teaches.

"Don't You just love the methods to my madness, Lord?"

"The methods that leave you drained and disillusioned, fatigued and frustrated? This chaos you create when you don't have to?"

"Yes, that would be me. But there's too much, Lord! How can I take care of everything at once?"

"You're asking the wrong question," He said.

"Again?"

"Afraid so. The question is only *where to begin*. The answer is an order that begins with *Me*, more of *Me*, and the rest will follow."

"And peace? Some peace in the chaos, please?"

"Gladly," He said. "I give you the peace of a life in order, where what you can't see is always more important than what you can. How's that?"

"Uh, could You simplify that for me please?"

He smiled and held my hand in His. "I just did."

"Fear not, for I am with you;
Be not dismayed, for I am your God.
I will strengthen you, Yes, I will help you,
I will uphold you with My righteous right hand."
Isaiah 41:10 NKJV

FINDING ORDER, FINDING PEACE If order is linked to peace, then how do we find it in all the jumbled, scattered, disorganized moments of our days? How can we clear a path for the promise? God says it's *more* before *less*, that order begins with Him, so we can start there. We can pause in the piles and get our lives under control—*His* control, not ours.

And the spiritual lessons will guide the physical ones. The universe may seem to conspire to bring only disruption and distortion to our lives, but it can't if we don't let it. We *choose* the amount of order in our lives, and that order leads to great peace. It's still there, under the mess, waiting for us.

ALMOST TIME. . . Let's follow a plan for a more orderly life, too, okay? Again, personalize it and claim it for your own. Look at your messy life and imagine the order God wants to bring to it. Allow Him to create order where there is none, to breathe peace where you need it.

Complete this sentence: I want more order in my life because

_____

_____

_____.

You may want to note the spiritual as well as the earthly parts of your life you feel are out of order. Or you may have a blanket plea because you can't find the words in the chaos of your mind. Either way, it's okay. Remember, the peace will find you. Now we can begin. Pray with me.

Another Fine Mess, Lord!

Lord, I pray for a life of order in my heart and home. I feel lost and inadequate to get a handle on everything my life throws at me. I don't know where to start, but You say start with You, so here I am. Help me bring order to my disorder and peace to my soul. Amen.

· · · · ·

This four-part plan works in your heart and in your home, too. You'll see the Lord even in the most unlikely places, restoring order when you ask.

1. Know What You Have
2. First Things First
3. Prepare the Way
4. Keep the Important Stuff Safe

Chapter 12

Know What You Have

Your eyes saw my unformed body.
All the days ordained for me
were written in your book
before one of them came to be.

PSALM 139:16 NIV

A couple of months after we bought our new car (okay, so it came to be several years deep into the last century, but it's new to me, and I can shift into reverse with only one hand, so I'm not complaining), the owner of the dealership where we traded called.

"Hey, this is Bighearted Bob," he said. Honest.

"I found some stuff under the seat of your vehicle you traded in. Do you want it?" he went on.

Oh, my, what'd he find? Not something embarrassing, I hope. That camera lens I lost eight years ago? (Please let it be the camera lens.) Money with my name on it? The fountain of youth?

"There's an old blanket, a windbreaker, a beach towel, and some garbage bags."

Story of my life, packed under a seat.

"Keep it," I told him. "I didn't know it was missing."

· · · · ·

When our lives are out of order, we lose track of a lot of things. We pack stuff away and then forget it's there. We leave remnants of our lives everywhere and then wonder why we can't get through one day intact, why even the most routine tasks become suitcases full of stress. When we can't even find the note we made to remind us of something we knew we'd forget, we begin to think it's time for another approach. There has to be a better way, a more peaceful way to make it through our days and, just maybe, through our lives. We need some help.

We have no peace because we always feel like the world we're holding up with our bony little fingers is just about to fall down on our heads. We seek escape and relief, and then we hear God say, *Let Me give you more.* We worry for a second, and then we realize He's taking the weight away the whole time He's giving us something more. He's making the world we're holding bearable because He's moving our focus to *what's holding us.*

GOD IS SO ORGANIZED God always knows where we are, what we need, what's going on in our lives. He doesn't have to look for us, sort through a stack of files to find us, or wonder if we're still here somewhere in the mess we've made. That kind of order to His work is the same kind of order we want. We can have it, in our spiritual life and our physical life, if we start where we are.

Disorder is depressing because everything seems so elusive, like we can't catch the chaos to corral it. Wouldn't you love to get up tomorrow and find everything in place and on time and nothing out of whack? Me, too, and there's something we can do today to get us headed in the right direction. We just need a map and a plan of where we're going. And here's the greatest part: We already know what it is.

When you try to organize your day, you have to know what commitments and appointments you have, right? The same is true for your spirit. You have to know what you have and what you don't.

You *have* the love of a God strong enough to bring order to whatever you've disordered. You *have* a God loving enough to forgive you wherever you've failed. You *have* a God patient enough to work you through whatever you don't understand.

Everything starts there, but sometimes we behave as if we don't have these wonders. We let too much else get in the way and forget or doubt the God who is strong enough to rescue us from all our disorder. Sometimes the chaos overwhelms us, and just like He said, the chaos on the inside is worse than that on the outside.

Before you even look at the mess of papers you haven't filed, look at the mess in your heart. Do you have fierce anger at someone else? At yourself? Do you battle resentment and envy? Do you have a bad attitude about your job or family? Do you have doubts about your purpose in life and how to fulfill it? Having what you don't need and missing what you *do* will keep the peace you want far, far away.

IT'S A LIST, A CHOICE Do you face each day knowing God is right beside you? Do you have the great belief in Him that frames everything else? Do you have the faith that can move mountains and the strength that can slay giants? It's more of *God first*, in these ways and many others, that brings you the order you want. Finding that order means filling the voids where you need God to be, allowing more of Him in your home and heart so you can keep what you need and discard the rest.

We need a place to start. Make a list of what you have and what you don't. We can't organize what we don't recognize, so here are a few questions to help you with your list. Remember: What you *need and don't have* is disrupting the order of your life, and what you *have and don't need* is disrupting the order of your life. Understand both, and order and peace will follow.

THIS I NEED

> *"I will not forget you!*
> *See, I have engraved you on the palms of my hands."*
> Isaiah 49:15–16 NIV

If we depend on our relationship with God to sustain us, we'll be able to have and to hold all the blessings He wants to give us. We'll meet each day with confidence and enthusiasm because we'll be prepared and organized, just like God. Here are a few things you'll need to live your great and wonderful life God has planned. And more He's made especially for you.

- Do you have a belief and acceptance in God's forgiveness? There's no way we can go forward if we don't let go of the past.

- Do you have an understanding of your place in God's heart? Can you begin to grasp the depth of His love for you?

- Do you have a thirst for more of Him in everything you do? We can't shut Him out of even the smallest place, because He cares about it all.

- Do you have a plan for the goals you've set? Are you learning to breathe in your water every day? Order comes from simplicity, and simplicity comes from order.

THIS I DON'T

> *For where you have envy and selfish ambition, there you find disorder and every evil practice.*
> JAMES 3:16 NIV

And what do you have that you'd be better off without? Like too much junk mail or too many recipes you'll never use (I'm clear on that one—why torture myself?), we usually have a destructive pile of "stuff under the seat" we'd rather not claim. When we know what we have and don't want, we can conquer it with what we do. Check out our list and add your own.

- Do you have a grudge against someone?

- Do you have worry and anxiety about your life?

- Do you have a bad habit or two you don't want?

- Do you have a hole in your heart that needs filling?

- Do you have resentment or envy burning inside?

- Do you have doubts or fears that paralyze you?

All of these "possessions" we hold in our hearts block the order and peace we need. But we can disown them if we choose. It doesn't matter how many items you have on your list. Because you put them there, on your list and in your heart, you can remove them. It's a matter of *more* of God and *less* of the rest.

A DAILY LIST Jesus proclaimed to the doubting Pharisees, easily and without reservation, "I know where I came from and where I am going" (John 8:14 NKJV). Can we? What can we add to our "coming from," and how does that affect our "going to" every day?

Can we approach each day with a little more understanding and wisdom than we had the day before? Can we come from a place of more compassion and humility each day, learning through the struggles we face to help others along the way? And are we going to a place closer to God every day, led by our study and submission to His Word? Are we going to a land of obedience and discovery, trusting the blessings to come because He said they would?

Are we daily leaving behind whatever stands between us and God—the list of what we don't need—and moving in the direction of His voice, to the list of what we do? Order doesn't come in a grand explosion, in some burst of brilliance, but from our daily walk, just a step a day following the map we know. Passage is a willing heart.

• • • • •

"Lord, You know what I have and what I don't want to have. Please help me bring order to the chaos."

"Of course. And know that I hold you in the palm of My hand, no matter how disorganized your world looks. Doesn't that clarify things a bit?"

"Sure does. Hey, I'm beginning to think simplifying my life helps me put everything in order. Did You plan that?"

"Could be. . . ." He winks at me, and I know there is more to come.

Another Fine Mess, Lord!

• • • • •

Keep me as the apple of your eye;
hide me in the shadow of your wings.

PSALM 17:8 NIV

Chapter 13

First Things First

"For your Father knows the things
you have need of before you ask Him."
MATTHEW 6:8 NKJV

This book you're holding is the first of its kind. No, you say, I've written others. That's true, but this one bears an irritating distinction: It's the first book I wrote with glasses on. While I was standing on my porch one day, trying to remember why I went out there, someone sneaked into my home and scrunched up all the print in my Bibles, moved the lines in my notebooks too close together, and dribbled fuzz I couldn't blink away over it all. I'd rather be audited than face that giant optometry machine that comes at me like something out of a horror movie, but I had to do it.

"Your eyes are in good shape," the doctor said, "except for your condition."

"I have a condition?"

A baby followed the last doctor's announcement that

I had a condition.

"You're over forty." He didn't even look up from my chart.

Well, so are you! my three adolescent brain cells still remaining wanted to snip at his head grayer than mine.

"Oh," I said intelligently.

Great, now I'm catalogued at the CDC? Officially old? The mean doctor offered no sympathy and just asked if I wanted lined or unlined bifocals.

Oh, let's don't hide my condition. Lined, please, preferably ones that'll glow in the dark. Unbelievable. Bifocals. But it was glasses first before any more writing. Or reading. Or sewing. Or eating. There's an order to everything, it seems.

• • • • •

The Lord's knowledge comes before our request, His desire to fill us before we even know we're empty. He knows the order our lives require because He created it.

God didn't wait until Adam and Eve were hungry to plant the garden. He didn't wait until He spilled the rain to tell Noah to build the ark. And He doesn't wait until we're drowning in guilt or pain to start manufacturing a little grace. He looks ahead, so He's never behind. We can be that organized, too, when we take care of first things first.

Do you know the aggravation when you need the phone or the scissors and can't find them? Do you know the chaos of lost records and missed appointments, hurried mornings and time-crunched work? What about the mess of mismanaged finances and misjudged circumstances? And that's just the disorder on the *outside* we have to deal with. What about the disorder on the *inside*, the pain in your heart when there's no calm, no security, no peace, when your mind is like a jigsaw puzzle with no picture on the box? When we follow God's lead and put first things first, we can restore the order. Let's look at a few examples.

TRUST BEFORE TRIAL

> *Consider it pure joy, my brothers,*
> *whenever you face trials of many kinds,*
> *because you know that the testing of your faith*
> *develops perseverance.*
> *Perseverance must finish its work so that you may be*
> *mature and complete, not lacking anything.*
> *If any of you lacks wisdom, he should ask God,*
> *who gives generously to all without finding fault,*
> *and it will be given to him.*
> *But when he asks, he must believe and not doubt,*
> *because he who doubts is like a wave of the sea,*
> *blown and tossed by the wind.*
>
> JAMES 1:2–6 NIV

We face fierce wind and wild seas in a lot of what we do. And we can panic about it, or we can work to get things in order with a trust in our God before we tackle the trials in our lives. He will never fail to show up when things get sticky in your life or in your heart. Are you facing a challenge at work, a confrontation with your teenager, a search for a new job? What about an illness, a breakup, a change in your life you didn't ask for? Yes, it's hard to find the traditional kind of "joy" we want in these situations, but we can forbid the disorder they threaten to create when we go to God with our trust first. He knows what's going on even when we don't.

We can trust that the guidance we need for *today* will arrive on time. Before we work to mend or correct or just survive the situation we're facing, we can strengthen our heart and remind ourselves of God's control. Then with our spirit in touch with His, we can live in this tangible world with the courage He provides. *Asking* if we'll get through our trials is unnecessary. *Thanking* God for the ways He'll help us through is the first step, and then *trusting* that help to arrive is the second. It's the *praise before the petition* that works every time.

COMPASSION BEFORE CRITICISM

> *Because of the LORD's great love we are not consumed,*
> *for his compassions never fail.*
> LAMENTATIONS 3:22 NIV

When we've failed, what does God do? He loves us and holds us close, and then He teaches us and shows us what we need to learn. But sometimes we forget to use that same compassion when we deal with others and hop straight to the criticism instead. We're especially prone to do this with those we love, usually out of our honest desire to help, but that's not the result. Instead, we don't feel any peace with ourselves because of the harsh way we've behaved, and those we love don't feel any peace because they asked for a loving hand and received a bitter heart instead.

And what about our own failures? We sure can dole out the criticism for ourselves, can't we? And again, there's no peace. But we can change all that with just a little compassion first. It won't mean we don't have to deal with whatever went wrong, but it will mean we can do it with a more peaceful heart. Try it now.

Think about some big mess you've made. How did you react? What was your first thought about yourself, about how you handled the situation? Now look at the mess again. What was going through your mind? What emotion led you to behave the way you did? Maybe you were hurting, maybe confused, maybe fatigued. Granting yourself a little compassion for the flawed human being you are doesn't mean that you excuse your behavior or justify your actions. It does mean that you'll better understand what caused you to fail, and when you're faced with a similar situation again, you'll be better equipped to deal with it because of what you've learned.

Compassion for yourself and those around you won't cost a thing, but it will bring a little more order and peace to your life. Take the time to follow God's example, and couple the teaching and training with care and compassion.

RESPONSIBILITY BEFORE REQUEST

> *Be completely humble and gentle;*
> *be patient, bearing with one another in love.*
>
> EPHESIANS 4:2 NIV

Seeking God's grace and redemption is the pattern for all

responsibility before request. We go to Him humble and bare, carrying our transgressions in our hands for Him to see. We know they're ours, and we take responsibility for them. Then we request the only salvation there is—His love. We do our part first. It's the same for all things inside our heart and out.

Sometimes dramas in our lives demand this practice. Even if you're the person least at fault in a situation, you have a part in it. When you acknowledge that, you're well on your way to finding peace. If you have a feud with an in-law, for example, think about what you've done in the past to add to it. Rectify that, and then ask for the other person's contribution to the truce. There's no need to try to "win," only to control what you can to find as much resolution and peace as possible. The order of responsibility before request works in relationships and in more tangible ways, too.

You can't expect your car to perform well unless you take care of it. You can't expect your body to stay well unless you protect and nourish it. You can't expect your children to respect themselves and others unless you model respect for them. You can't expect your spouse to know your feelings unless you tell him. Do your part in these situations and thousands like them, and feel the order take over every time.

• • • • •

With these examples, and even the everyday routine

messes like lost scissors and missed deadlines, it's a simple matter of *thinking* before *acting*. *Think* of where you'll keep the scissors and return them there every time you use them. *Think* of your deadline and do the work for it before you do other work that can wait. *Think* of God's faithfulness to you before you fight your battles. *Think* of reaching out with a caring hand before giving instruction. *Think* of the work you'll do yourself before asking others.

We want to remember in all activity to "do the first works" (Revelation 2:5 NKJV) of loving God and loving others. We order our lives well when we ask, "How can I reflect God's love in this work?" I'm sure you have plenty of goals that fit this pattern.

As we learn to look at all we've disordered by forgetting *first things first*, then we can start again. We can restore the order we seek by following God's example. Then we're ready to prepare the way for more of His blessings to follow.

• • • • •

Recall a few times you brought disorder to your life by ignoring the importance of first things first. How would you handle those situations differently today?

_____

_____

_____

_____

_____

Another Fine Mess, Lord!

Make yourself a few "think first" notes and post them on your refrigerator, your computer, in your car—wherever you'll see them often. Record how the notes help you bring more order to your days.

_____

_____

_____

_____

_____

_____

Chapter 14

Prepare the Way

"I am the voice of one calling in the desert,
'Make straight the way for the Lord.'"
JOHN 1:23 NIV

Before Jesus walked on earth, God prepared His way. He didn't have to say, "Whoa, hold on a minute, Son," while He found someone to announce His coming. The plan and purpose God decreed happened the way He ordered it. He knew what He needed, and He sent John first. We can follow His example and feel more in control when we prepare the way for our plans and purposes. We'll do nothing so grand as become the foreteller of Jesus, but we can organize the work of our hearts and our homes when we learn from everything before us. We usually learn a lot from what doesn't work.

We learn from those times our dreams died because we weren't prepared. Maybe you've known one of those times? Have you failed to reach a goal because you never made the way for it? Have you taken on a project at work and then failed because you didn't prepare? Have you stayed in a job or house that didn't fit because you never prepared for something better?

It's when we ignore the work that it never gets done. Preparing the way isn't difficult, but we tend to avoid it sometimes because we're afraid. We needn't be. It's all part of the "relationship before the rescue," loving God first, working next. And it comes filled with peace when we get our lives in order. Like everything else we're learning here, it starts with what we can't see.

GOD'S WAY Preparing the way in your life is really preparing yourself for God's way into your soul. Each day, choose to do at least one thing to get you closer to the person you want to be. Here's a guide to help, no matter how disordered your life is.

- *Prepare your heart—with prayer and expectation of God's touch.* What mess can you and God undo today? How can you praise and honor Him in your actions today? What opportunities will He present, and how will you respond? Thank your Lord in advance for walking with you through every second of your life, and listen when He tells you He'll never go away.

- *Prepare your mind—with prayer and expectation of God's touch.* Look at the effects of your choices and see where you've chosen wisely and where you've chosen unwisely. Accept all that's happened and open your mind to what is yet to be. We have to learn as we go, and God stays close to guide us so we don't have to retrace our steps.

- *Prepare your will—with prayer and expectation of God's touch.* We are most at peace when our will coincides with God's. Ask Him to help you become more obedient, more receptive to His plans for you, more secure in what He tells you. Like an ivy vine around a trellis, you can bend your will to God's when you know which way to go.

• • • • •

Living your life as an example of God's grace and abiding care brings order to your life because you are a walking picture of what comes first. You fell, that's true, but He rescued you. He prepared for that order when He planned His grace and decided He would grant you His forgiveness. If you go to Him humble and sincere, He will withhold nothing. That unchanging fact brings order to everything else.

So even if you've made a mess of things in the past (like all of us have), you can restore order today because God is forever there to answer your call, like He has been for thousands of years: "I will heal their waywardness and love them freely, for my anger has turned away from them" (Hosea 14:4 NIV). Show His grace to those around you, and help them restore order in their lives, too.

ORDERING THEM GONE The intangible things we harbor in our hearts live there and create destruction until we get rid of them. We can't prepare for anything when we hold more of something we don't need instead of more of God. But we can rejoice. There is an order to overcoming the greed or despair or envy or fear that prevents us from reaching our goals and living in peace. We get out of order following these "other lords" that steal us away from our God.

LORD, you establish peace for us;
all that we have accomplished you have done for us.
O LORD, our God, other lords besides you have ruled over us,
but your name alone do we honor.

ISAIAH 26:12–13 NIV

The path to the Lord's order for handling the everyday-ness of our disordered lives is there, under the mess. It's like reclaiming the garage you've abandoned to junk—there's something far better for its use, and you allow it when you prepare the way. Your heart is the same. Let's look at one of the most damaging obstacles preventing our peace and see how we can choose something much better.

PREPARE THE WAY FOR A LIFE WITHOUT WORRY

The LORD is my light and my salvation; whom shall I fear?
The LORD is the strength of my life; of whom shall I be afraid?
Though an army may encamp against me, my heart shall not
fear; though war may rise against me, in this I will be confident.

PSALM 27:1, 3 NKJV

Worry is a habit and a choice. I should know. I've had years of practice, along with years of trying to learn how to overcome it. I've tried logic and statistics and tricks of all kinds, but they don't work. Something does, though, and—again—it's about more of God, about more *release* to God. When we release our worry to Him, we don't have to just say, "Okay, have at it, Lord," and walk around with a fragile faith, afraid to peek and see if He really took it. Instead, we instantly get something wonderful in return for our release. With our hearts wide open instead of closed in fear, God pours in His love, direction, compassion, and comfort. Our focus changes from our *worry* to our *Lord*.

The pain and doubt are shoved out of the way when, in one breath, we prepare the way for God to enter, when we trust first in His command and control of our lives and remind ourselves of His perfect record. He has never failed to come near when we've asked. And all the worrying in the world will never produce the amount of peace one tiny moment of releasing our worry to God will. It takes practice, but that's okay—the Lord is the world's greatest and most patient coach. Releasing our worry to God becomes a habit and a choice, too. I should know.

The pattern is the same for all that hurts, more of God so there's less of the pain. If there's anger in your heart, make way for God's understanding and forgiveness to become your own. If there's fear in your heart, make way for God's courage and boldness to become your own. If there's resentment in your heart, make way for God's compassion and faithfulness to become your own. Prepare the way.

ORDER IN YOUR HOME Learning a better order of things in your heart helps you learn a better order of things in your home. You can welcome peace to the everyday life you touch when you take the time to know what you have and put first things first.

PREPARE THE WAY FOR A LIFE OF CALM You create order by preparing the way for a smoother beginning to your day. If your mornings usually consist of struggles with your children, a fight with your closet, a search for whatever you need for work or school, and the absolute absence of even a moment with God, there's no peace. You know that. You might blame it on too much to do or someone else's bad habits, and we all know how hard it is to coordinate the chaos when several people are involved. But there's much you can do to fix what touches you. That's where the order begins.

What do you know you have to do in the mornings? How much of it can you do the night before? Help your kids check a "ready for tomorrow" list and prepare what they can before bedtime. Do you find clothes that need mending when you're in a rush? Tend to those things as they happen, and have a couple backup plans for wardrobe emergencies. Nothing ready for lunch? Give it some thought the night before. Again, it's simply thinking ahead so you're never behind.

PREPARE THE WAY FOR A LIFE OF RESPONSIBILITY You create order by preparing the way for more peace about your money. Our lives always feel out of order when we're concerned about finances. And unless hundred-dollar bills start showing up in your laundry like mismatched socks, you have to take responsibility for how you manage the money in your life. Remember, it's not about the *conditions* you face but the *choices* you make. You start today to understand your money and to allocate it wisely. There's no mystery to it. You do your best to fix what touches you. That's where the order begins.

There's no peace when we're struggling to pay bills or creating a mountain of credit card debt. *I know, but what do I do now if that's already the case?* you ask. You tend to first things first. You eliminate what you don't need or can't afford, and you make responsible choices about what to do with the money you have. It's not hard to understand or a tough pattern to follow. If you choose to go on vacation with money you need for your mortgage payment, you're only preparing the way for more stress and disorder. The pattern is the same in big expenditures or small ones. Thinking through the situation *before* you spend your money helps you see what action to take. Choose wisely and order prevails.

PREPARE THE WAY FOR A LIFE OF JOY You create order by preparing the way for more enjoyment of the events of your life. That sounds strange, doesn't it? What does order have to do with joy? The answer is "everything." Think about it. You know Christmas comes on the same day every year. Yet if you wake up on December 20 and behave as if the event were just added to your calendar, you'll probably be facing it with anything but joy and peace.

The same is true for birthdays, graduations, anniver-saries. . . anything. You won't know what you have or what you need for the occasion, and the time before it will be filled with stress and chaos, as everything has to be done quickly—or important items get left out—because you didn't prepare the way that allows for peace. No, you can't foresee every crisis or have the perfect Christmas turkey, and you don't have to. You only need to fix what touches you. That's where the order begins.

The more you prepare ahead of time for an event, the more likely you are to be relaxed when it occurs. If you plan to take care of responsibilities ahead of time, at your leisure, you can easily work around snags or delays, set aside money or supplies, and allow your creativity and excitement to build as you prepare. There will always be "last-minute" things to do, but most of what we do doesn't have to be that way. We can do much of it in an order of our own making, and joy always follows.

"No eye has seen, no ear has heard, no mind has conceived
what God has prepared for those who love him."
1 CORINTHIANS 2:9 NIV

• • • • •

The path to more order and peace is the same no matter what the situation, no matter if it happens in your home and you can touch it, or if it happens in your heart and you can feel it. Making sense of the chaos in your life brings order, and it's not complicated unless you choose to make it so. There's always less disorder when there's more of God in everything you do. Know that, put it first.

· · · · ·

How will you prepare your *heart, mind,* and *will* for more of God today?

_____

_____

_____

What destructive "other lords" do you need to order gone from your heart?

_____

_____

_____

Choose an area of your life that needs better preparation. What will you do to bring more order into the situation today, this week, this month?

_____

_____

_____

Chapter 15

Keep the Important Stuff Safe

Above all else, guard your heart, for it is the wellspring of life.
PROVERBS 4:23 NIV

Where is God's grace and love? Where is His forgiveness and guidance? Where are His arms to wrap you when you need to feel Him close? Everything important and essential is always safe, right where He needs it so He can give it to you. He doesn't need a day or two to look for something. Can we make the same claim?

Can we find last year's tax returns? The safe–deposit box key? And where is our grace for others, our fairness and compassion, our love that exemplifies the Lord's? We can follow God's example and keep the things we need the most safe and close to us, in our hearts and in our homes. Then we eliminate a lot of time and frustration because there's no frantic searching—there's only peace because we have our lives organized God's way.

Part 3

THE THINGS YOU CAN'T SEE. . .

"O you of little faith, why did you doubt?"
MATTHEW 14:31 NKJV

When Peter released his doubt, he walked on water. When he gave in to the fear and allowed the doubt to consume him, he began to sink. But Jesus saved him. Jesus caught him and then taught him. He does the same for us.

When I'm faced with a tough challenge, sometimes I get scared, too. Can I do my part? Will I make it in time? I can feel myself sinking, sometimes just like Peter. The "boisterous wind" around me is a circumstance in my life, but my response is the same: "Lord, save me! Save me from this doubt that consumes me."

If Peter had kept his faith in Jesus, he wouldn't have thought too much about his gravity-defying feat. I know it works, because I practiced it throughout the writing of this book. I believed that if I could keep my faith in Christ, I wouldn't think too much about the days dissolving under me as the deadline rushed in.

"Lord," I prayed early in my work, "please help me with this book." I needed to feel Him close to me, guiding me. And He said, "Do you doubt I'll hold you up?" I wanted to say, "No, I don't doubt!" but the wind would blow again.

And then I was reminded that it wasn't the wind that made Peter fall, but his *change of focus*. My prayer was backward! Instead of "Please help me with this work," I could pray, "Please hold me in Your hand." If my focus was on the Lord's power and strength instead of my fear and weakness, there truly was no reason to doubt. He holds me up because He knows the winds of my world will always blow strong. And I can walk on the water when I remember He's stronger.

WRITE IT DOWN You can bring great order to your home when you keep the important physical things safe, too. To help you remember where to find both the tangible and intangible items and bring more peace to your life, make yourself a graph with four columns and as many rows as you need.

The first column is filled with the tangible things you need to keep track of: important papers (tax records and birth certificates), extra keys, emergency cash, address book, important phone numbers, batteries, medications, glasses, checkbook, scissors and tape, stamps and envelopes for paying bills, a calendar with important dates noted—you get the idea, whatever you regularly misplace.

The next column is the location for those things—desk, shoebox in the hall closet, safe–deposit box, et cetera. When you decide on a place for something, keep it there, safe.

The next column is filled with the intangible things you need to keep track of: God's love, compassion, forgiveness, and patience; your goals, sense of humor, compassion for others, and humility.

The final column tells you where to find those things. This part is really simple: every space is the same because they all live in your heart. Keep them there, safe.

Part 3

• • • • •

My mom cross-stitched a picture for me that sits on my desk where I see it every day. It is a yellow rose in an oval of green with these words: *Lord, help me to remember that nothing can happen today that together You and I can't handle.* Whether I'm struggling with something too big for me or just plodding through the everyday, the words remind me to keep my faith in God safe and close so that I go to it *first* and order everything that follows afterward. If I lose that faith, disorder prevails because I've lost a most important thing. Despite any complications of the world, my faith must remain. I'm nothing without it, and there is no peace outside it.

> *"As the rain and the snow come down from heaven,*
> *and do not return to it without watering the earth*
> *and making it bud and flourish,*
> *so that it yields seed for the sower and bread for the eater,*
> *so is my word that goes out from my mouth:*
> *It will not return to me empty, but will accomplish what I*
> *desire and achieve the purpose for which I sent it."*
>
> ISAIAH 55:10–11 NIV

Chapter 16

Peace in the Mess—
Your Own Little Red Wagon

I'm sure I had a real little red wagon once, but it was the metaphorical kind I heard about all my growing-up years. Every time I'd want to leave my work undone and meddle in someone else's, I'd hear my grandmother, whether she was there or not, remind me, "Tend to your own little red wagon." It was all she had to say. In my mind, I could see a wagon with my name on it, full and needing my attention. That command put everything back in order.

Make it your ambition to lead a quiet life,
to mind your own business and to work with your hands.
1 Thessalonians 4:11 niv

Paul's words speak to us today, as well. If we want to have order in our lives, we must do what we can to create and protect it. When our ambition is clear, order follows.

How do we "lead a quiet life" in the chaotic world

around us? Even a dinner out is spoiled by ringing cell phones, and our own responsibilities seem to scream at us nonstop. But it doesn't matter. The quiet we crave is within our control because it's a quiet of *peace*, sustained by our breathing connection to the Lord. It's the life God's prepared for us, full of Him and quiet in the way that shows, instead of yells, what it's about. As we seek order, we find quiet.

And this kind of quiet is so encapsulated and cocooned by God's love and grace that nothing touches it. This kind of quiet is about being reverent and grateful, respectful of all the Lord has placed before you, while gladly accepting your part in taking care of all you've been given. This kind of quiet is about relying on God, about living as a testament to His power and presence, about moving everything you don't need out of your heart and getting what you do need in order.

Take the time to look at your days. How much is noise and chaos, both in your home and in your mind? How much of what you think about and look at every day is loud and bothersome? Work to rid yourself of everything that isn't soothing and restorative to your soul. Lead the quiet life God's designed for you—one so full of Him that it keeps everything damaging away. It's the strongest quiet you could ever imagine.

To "mind your own business" may sound like a statement of inaction, but it's quite the opposite. Though it sounds like only an admonition to watch our manners and refrain from passing judgment, it's so much more. This command teaches us the individuality of our faith. The responsibility to ourselves is there in everything, from what we think, to what we say, to what we do. The charge is one filled with action and attention, with preparing the way for the order and peace of God.

The Lord gave you this life for a reason. He gave it to you with gifts and abilities and talents and a mind and a heart to follow your dreams. He didn't put you here indiscriminately, but *purposefully*. And there is no one on this planet who can do what He needs from you but *you*. The responsibility for your business begins and ends with *you*.

Every day, ask yourself if you're minding your business. Are you going about God's work in everything you do, in the way you're spending your valuable time? Are you pursuing your goals? Are you developing your gifts and becoming the witness you want to be? Are you growing and learning every day, feeling like you're sitting on the top of a waterspout that's just shooting higher and higher with joy and possibility? If not, then you're not minding your business. If not, then your life is out of order because your business is God's business. Tend to that first.

Another part of minding our own business involves opening up to God and being willing to listen to what He says. We can pray, "Search me, O God, and know my heart; test me and know my anxious thoughts" (Psalm 139:23 NIV). It's your business to take what the Lord reveals to you and do with it what He directs. And how do you do that in practical ways every day? You tend to what is yours—filling your heart, growing your soul, fighting your battles, counting your blessings. In every situation you find yourself, look at your choices and touch what is yours to touch. Clarify, explain, teach, forgive, share, love, understand—whatever is yours to do, do it. See your life as the gift it is and don't waste it. Your little red wagon is waiting.

Our walk with God is spiritual and surreal, but it's also tangible, a walk of works you couldn't hold in if you wanted to. And order comes from resourcefully putting this part of your journey into practice as you "work with your hands."

Why is this point important enough to come like a command, as important as the mental work of learning about your Lord? It's important because God wants you to feel His touch on you and then extend it to others. When you work with your hands—when you interact with your world—you touch His love and His grace, for yourself and others. You see the opportunities God puts in your path and find a way to turn whatever you face into something for Him. I have no idea what's in your path, but you do, and it can be anything. The work you find to do is the work of the Lord.

God gave you the ability to think and to find solutions, but He won't do the work for you. That's your *job*, to touch the world around you in a productive, fruitful, and resourceful manner, by taking care of first things first and meeting your responsibilities. And you can do that every day, even as lofty as it sounds, because it's the simple work you do that connects you with God—finding gratitude in a challenge, extending grace in an argument, sharing your knowledge with someone who wants to learn, giving your time to someone who needs a companion. Those actions put order into your life by reminding you where your strength lies, where your future will be—all wrapped up in the God who never refuses to work with His hands on *you*.

No matter what you do, there is nothing menial or grand in any work, because it's all given with the same heart, fills your same little red wagon. Sweeping the floor is the same as building a cathedral when you do it with the pleasure and the purpose of serving the Lord. But "work" is more than labor. It's not just your job or your chores or your goals. It's the connection you feel when you touch a part of this world and change it. To "work with your hands" is to take something and make it better, to leave something repaired or renewed when you're done. That may be a friend's house or a friend's heart; it doesn't matter.

And whatever you do, whether in word or deed,
do it all in the name of the Lord Jesus,
giving thanks to God the Father through him.
COLOSSIANS 3:17 NIV

Create something and know you're alive. Share what you've been chosen to receive. Use what you have in your life to work for God. Take everything you've been given, all of the talents you have, and distribute them along your path. Work with what you have—your hands, your mind, your abilities—to touch your world and touch others. Your little red wagon overflows, and you are blessed.

Lord, Your order to my life is amazing. You give me what I need and help me rid myself of what I don't. I needn't live in chaos and stress when I prepare and protect my steps with you. Please help me keep order in all this complicated world throws at me by learning from Your example. You love me first and always. May I remember to love You first and always, and everything else will follow. Thank You for creating my little red wagon and filling it with Your order and peace. Amen.

• • • • •

My Daily Affirmation of Order

My life is in order when my life is in God.

Part 4

Insight in the Confusion

Let the morning bring me
word of your unfailing love,
for I have put my trust in you.
Show me the way I should go,
for to you I lift up my soul.

PSALM 143:8 NIV

"Lord, please grant me insight for my life."
"Beloved, I already have."

Chapter 17

Insight Waiting

"You can complicate any decision; you know that?" the Lord asked me rather bluntly.

"Well. . .yeah. . .but some choices are tough," I pleaded.

"No, all choices are the same. Learn the way to your insight. I've given you a map, and the landmarks never change."

"Hmm, sounds doable. Go with me?"

"Don't you know—you can't go without Me."

What a relief.

Humble yourselves, therefore, under God's mighty hand,
that he may lift you up in due time.
Cast all your anxiety on him because he cares for you.

1 PETER 5:6–7 NIV

Sometimes harder to find than simplicity or order is the knowledge of what we should do. Do you always feel you have piercing wisdom and perfect insight about everything in your life? No? Me neither, even though I wish I did. Only God knows all the answers, but I've learned something wonderful: He's willing to share.

He's ready for our pleas and protests, our questions and confusion. He's not worried, because He's prepared with a guide to help us make decisions in our lives. We can ask ourselves a few key questions and find the answers we need, not because it's easy, but because His infinite instruction makes it make sense in our finite world.

The Lord meets us in our everydayness with practical guidance wrapped in His love. You have the insight you need in abundance, so don't ever worry about that. Others who appear sure and at peace with their decisions don't have anything you don't, except years of practice that have made finding their insight a little easier.

Yes, God is spirit and soul and feeling and heart, but He is also a brilliant action plan that breathes. And in every breath is His love for us.

The LORD's unfailing love surrounds the man who trusts in him.
PSALM 32:10 NIV

· · · · ·

I can remember watching television when I was a little girl, intrigued by characters who could read minds or see into the future. I wanted that power! And wouldn't it be great? Of course, but that's not to be. What we do have, though, is a God-given intuition. And I don't mean something vague or enigmatic. I mean the *insight* God built into us from the beginning. It's waiting for us. When we choose to claim it and let it possess us, we stand amazed at its clarity and accuracy. We know how to navigate through the minefields of a complicated world by drawing on its power, a power personal and true to exactly what we need. Sure, we have to develop our insight, nurture and protect it, but we can always *trust* it, because it comes from God. He would not allow the questions if we couldn't find the answers.

And the finding is a joint venture. We don't learn anything on our own. Our insight within is paired with the wisdom of God to guide us faithfully every day. It's both a journey and a joy to hold and practice this amazing gift. And when you do, I guarantee you'll never wring your hands and say you don't know what to do again. Your insight is that strong—and available.

Like Solomon, we can humbly ask for wisdom in making our decisions. "So give your servant a discerning heart to govern your people and to distinguish between right and wrong" (1 Kings 3:9 NIV). We may never lead a nation, but we can lead our lives with God-given insight to bring us peace, that we may "understand what the Lord's will is" (Ephesians 5:17 NIV).

ALMOST TIME. . . Our plan to uncover our insight consists of four points. Some decisions may require more attention to one point than another, and you'll know where your heart is leading you. The plan works in all situations you'll face. God moves ever closer, and the learning never ends. Start now.

Complete this sentence: I want more insight in my life because

_____

_____

_____

Is there an immediate trouble hurting you? Or do you feel lost and don't know where to turn next? Have you trusted your insight in the past but now can't seem to find it? Don't worry. No mess is too much for God's wisdom, and He will grant you the insight and guidance you need when you ask. Now we can begin. Pray with me.

Lord, I pray for the touch of Your wisdom on my troubled heart. You know how much I struggle with decisions and, at the same time, how much I only want to do Your will. Please guide me in every choice, help me hear You, enable me to understand, and grant me courage to follow. Please help me find the peace that great insight brings. Amen.

• • • • •

Now you're ready to breathe the great insight of your Lord. It's waiting for you.

1. Be True to Who You Are
2. Do What You Know
3. Learn What You Don't Know
4. Seek Peace

Chapter 18

Be True to Who You Are

Your word is a lamp to my feet and a light for my path.
PSALM 119:105 NIV

The Lord Himself is a living example of this step of our plan. He is *always* true to who He is because He can be no other way. When we feel uncomfortable with a decision, it's likely because we're not being true to who we are. You know those times, the "What am I doing here?" desperation when you've made a choice that hurts you now. Big or small, the pattern is the same.

And so is the result: the lack of peace in your heart. If you want to know if you'll find peace in a decision, ask yourself if the choice is true to who you are. Let's look at an example.

Attending a staff meeting and calling clients may be parts of your job you have to endure. Maybe you don't enjoy these activities, but there's enough of your job that you do love to make you want to keep it. You feel fulfilled, and you're doing something you enjoy—it fits who you are. But what if it's not? What if the meetings are just the worst part of a nearly unbearable situation?

If so, your discomfort is trying to tell you something, and you don't need supernatural powers to figure it out. We can blame others when we complicate our lives with situations that itch like poison oak, or we can allow our *insight* to possess us and God's wisdom to direct us to a place that suits us, a place of peace. And that place is one of truth, because truth leads to simplicity, remember? It's all part of God's plan to keep us out of a mess—or as in my case most of the time, to help us out of a mess. It's all part of our quest for peace.

> *Blessed is the man who finds wisdom,*
> *the man who gains understanding,*
> *for she is more profitable than silver*
> *and yields better returns than gold.*
> PROVERBS 3:13–14 NIV

ALWAYS LEARNING. . . What if you *are* in a place that doesn't fit? Does that mean you should quit your job tomorrow? I doubt it. Finding peace often begins with understanding the lack of it. If you've put yourself in a place you don't want to be, let it teach you. It's not a waste, just a stopover on a much grander journey. From the unpeaceful places, we learn much. And that's okay.

Your great life begins here and now with building your relationship with God—your *unique* relationship. Learning to choose the right circumstances that allow you to do your unique work takes time and practice. And we make a lot of mistakes along the way. Because even though we learn more about who we are every day, our complicated world weighs heavily on us and we stumble under the strain. But you know what? It's not in vain. We learn something to help us the *next* time we have to choose—that's insight in action.

This part of our plan is really a process, because we grow and change and God finds new ways to make our world brighter every day. If we want insight, we must stay in tune with who we are and who God is creating us to be. Then we can freely live the great life that's only ours. And that brings us back to the beginning—to building that unique relationship with God.

"You know so much of this already," the Lord says.

"Huh? I have insight already?"

"Of course. Sometimes it's after the fact that you realize it, but you know when you've been true to yourself and when you haven't."

"Boy, do I. I'd like to know *before* the fact. Any pointers?"

"Ask. Trust. Believe. Learn as you go, My child. Go with *Me*. That is all the insight you need."

I feel wiser already.

· · · · ·

The Lord was so right about knowing when we're in the wrong place. It's that uneasy feeling in your middle when you've put yourself in somebody else's little red wagon, when you're living a life of lies and pretense. We know that place because there's no peace in our hearts. We know because, at the end of the day, no matter how hard we work, we can't look back and say, "That was good."

Aaron knew the power of God personally. He was a spiritual man, a high priest, yet he made a decision against all the insight he'd known and began a life inconsistent with who he was. Did he give in to peer pressure? Did he think he could lie and God wouldn't notice? Did he abandon his goal? "He took what they handed him and made it into an idol cast in the shape of a calf, fashioning it with a tool" (Exodus 32:4 NIV). Did Aaron ask for God's guidance, trust Him, believe His promises?

Maybe you've built your own golden calf once or twice, giving in to others' pressures or trying to be something you're not, living a life that isn't yours. And why? The loss is so great when we substitute a faulty insight for our own that comes from God. That's no way to our own promised land. The peace is gone.

LEARNING MORE. . . But don't despair. While we will always have quandaries and queries in this complicated world, we also have a base, a center that never changes. We just have to let it possess us when so much else is trying to. The rest of the world may be totally confused, but we don't have to be, even if we're in the midst of the confusion. Our insight may seem fractured and scattered, like split kindling in a tornado, but we can simply wait for the noise in our heads to stop, collect the pieces of *our* truth, reassemble, and start again. We seek the congruency, and order and insight follow.

Sometimes it takes us awhile to understand our insight and God's leading. Even Moses was nervous, struggling to make the right decision. "O Lord, please send someone else to do it" (Exodus 4:13 NIV), he asked God. The Lord responded to Moses' fear and understood his human insecurities. But He wouldn't relent. I think He calls us the same way today because His work changes but never ends.

With great courage and honor, Moses trusted his insight and fulfilled his mission. When Moses decided to be true to who he was, his world changed. The outside may have looked anything but peaceful, but he had the peace of God in his heart forever. Okay, the sea has already parted. The tablets are done. But your choices today reach far and wide, too.

> *The man who plants and the man who waters*
> *have one purpose, and each will be rewarded*
> *according to his own labor.*
> *For we are God's fellow workers;*
> *you are God's field, God's building.*
>
> 1 CORINTHIANS 3:8–9 NIV

Let's say you do know you're in the wrong job. Don't panic—that's the beginning point, not the ending. Then you can work where you are to meet your responsibilities while you find the job that fits. By ordering your decision with first things first, you allow God to breathe a little peace your way. The daily trials remain, but your steps on the path you want to follow are lighted.

Things seem simple—you've made your decision, and now you'll just follow through. The insight you need possesses you and guides you when you allow it. Following your heart is not selfish, but self-fulfilling, because you're in touch with God's plan, with His answers, with the insight He provides.

AHH. . . *But what about the times I make the wrong decision?* you say. *What about the times I put myself in a bad place? What about the times I see no guiding signs? Or when I behave like Aaron? What then?* Then we still have God, close to us when we're weak, scared, influenced. We're imperfect, and the Lord understands.

Peter, the disciple Jesus commissioned to feed His sheep (John 21:18), even faltered when he three times denied Christ. There was probably nothing he could have done that was more inconsistent with who he was. Yet great insight followed Peter's lack because he still chose his Lord. And *that* is the hope and redemption for us all.

When we're weak and have lost our way, we need the Lord to guide us back on course. And He responds. It's when we stagger that He steps in. Yes, we make bad choices, squash opportunities, misplace our trust. But Peter showed us that's not the end. With every *"oops!"* there's an *"ahh. . ."*

If we never knew thirst, how could we appreciate

the quench of water? If we never knew hurt, how could we appreciate the healing of God? If we never knew complicated, how could we appreciate the peace of simplicity?

We learn, we learn again, and we learn more. It's what we do, over and over, learning to walk hand in hand with God through all the decisions we face. And we learn who we are.

WHO ARE YOU? So whom did the Lord make when He made you? Let me start, okay? No, I'm not clairvoyant, but I do know these things:

- You are *loved*, because God's heart is too big to let go of you when you ask Him to hold you.
- You are *capable*, because His gifts don't skip anyone, and if you need a gift, you have it.
- You are *trusted*, because God created a mission just for you, and it's waiting for you to claim it.

Write for yourself here more of who you are:

I am _____. I am _____.

I am _____. I am _____.

I am _____. I am _____.

WHERE ARE YOU? Think of a situation you're in now

that doesn't fit. How'd you get there? Did you feel "in your gut" that it might not fit and yet went ahead anyway? (We do that sometimes.) If that's the case, what cues did you miss or ignore? Or if you can't explain how you got there and sort of just "evolved" into a place without peace, why are you continuing to live there?

Now think of a situation that *does* fit. Maybe it's your job, your church, your marriage, a friendship, volunteer work, or the way you spend your Saturday afternoons. Everything is a choice, big or small, and they all add up to your life. How did you arrive at these choices that fit who you are? How did you find peace in them? What about these situations makes them work for you and deepen your relationship with God? Learn from them.

WHO WILL YOU BECOME? Now, think for a moment about a difficult decision you're presently facing. Remember it as we work through this part of our book. Before we get into our other steps, what does your intuition tell you about this choice? Which parts of the situation fit who you are and which ones don't? If you had to choose today, what would you do? Do you believe you have the insight to make the better choice? God does.

He trusts you to choose well for yourself, and you do that by being true to Him and who you are in Him, to His workmanship—following His Word and walking your way to the great purpose He made for you. You can feel that; I know you can. Your insight is inside, always guiding you, just like God. Use it well.

Another Fine Mess, Lord!

Do your best to present yourself to God as one approved,
a workman who does not need to be ashamed and
who correctly handles the word of truth.

2 TIMOTHY 2:15 NIV

· · · · ·

"Couldn't I just have a little of that ESP or ride in a time machine just once so I'd know what to do now and then, Lord?" I offered.

"Nope, sorry. It doesn't work that way."

"Well, how *does* it work? How can I become wise like You? A little less *oops* would be nice."

"Simple. Be who I made you to be. Then do what you know, learn what you don't. This isn't as complicated as you make it sound."

"Are You sure?"

"Believe Me, I know complicated. I've watched you create havoc and desperation and chaos too many times to count because you failed to do what you knew and learn what you didn't. Want to reminisce about those times?"

"No, really, that's okay," I blurted out at Mach speed. "Can we just start from now? Can You help me see the lighted path now?"

"*Now* is my favorite time."

Chapter 19

Do What You Know

So then, just as you received Christ Jesus as Lord,
continue to live in him.

COLOSSIANS 2:6 NIV

Our insight is born of who we are and nurtured in what we know. Every choice and action, every encounter with God, and every misguided attempt to live without Him teaches us. We grow and learn, and if we pay attention, we can almost feel the insight we crave stretch and expand to fill our needs. There is nothing too hard for God and no decision we should fear. If we feel inadequate to solve our problems, we shouldn't, because we can always *do what we know*. Living in our Lord is what we know.

"There's no need to treat every decision like a star or a snowflake. They're all the same," He said.

"I wouldn't want to disagree with You on that point, Lord, but I can't think of any decision I've had to make twice. Each one is always tougher and more difficult than the one before it."

"No, the details are different, maybe, but the process is the same, just like Me. And when you do what you know, every time, you're halfway there. See? The same."

"No, sorry, I don't see, but that's okay? You'll show me?"

"I show you every moment, My dear one. I make the same decision every day, to love you no matter what. Your decision is to trust Me or not. And the insight follows."

Who'd have guessed?

• • • • •

The Lord's words bring us back again to building that most special relationship with Him. If it's insight and peace we want, we find it with *more of Him* first. He's right about all our decisions being the same after all—either to let His wisdom in or shut Him out. And in our complicated world, that one decision presents itself in about a million different ways. Ever human and flawed, we make a lot of bad calls as we learn how to make better ones. The insight follows, though, because much of it comes from those messes we've made in the past, and the rest comes from the love of a forgiving God.

If it's true that good judgment comes from experience and experience comes from bad judgment, then some of us (namely, me) should have enough good judgment to last a lifetime. Maybe you feel like you could join me. Good judgment comes from paying attention to what we know, what we've learned through our poor choices and misfitting obligations. Even when we've failed to do what we know before, we can always choose to do what we know next time. Knowledge is power, the saying goes. Let's find out.

THE KNOWLEDGE OF BEGINNING The people in Joseph's day may have thought he made a poor decision when he married a pregnant Mary. But Joseph didn't. He was probably scared, but he trusted what he knew to guide him through what he'd have to learn. All insight begins with the *knowledge of beginning*—with doing what we know closest to our hearts and homes.

Paul cautioned against giving power to church leaders who couldn't lead their own homes well. "If a man does not know how to rule his own house, how will he take care of the church of God?" (1 Timothy 3:5 NKJV). If we don't do what we know in our routine, everyday lives, how can we learn what we *don't* know?

Rarely are we faced with a decision for which we have no precedent. Sure, the scenarios may seem complicated, but our mission remains the same—be true to who we are and follow God's example in our choices. We know the Lord has never misrepresented Himself to us. He has never claimed to be something He isn't. We know He will do what He says He will. If I decide to buy something I know I can't afford to impress a friend, I'm not "ruling my own house" well. I'm not doing what I know, and I'll only have to relearn lessons of truth and order again before I can find peace.

But what if you're already in a job you hate? What if you already have obligations and burdens because of poor choices? It doesn't matter. Whenever you decide to claim the insight within you, that's the beginning. *That's* when you make the decision to do what you know.

If you don't want your job but can't leave it right now, realize you have to pay your bills and face your responsibilities today. Be the best employee you can while you develop a plan for a better job by *learning what you don't know* (the next point in our plan). Deciding that you need peace in this kind of situation is a wonderful beginning. Pursue it without pause.

Again, the Lord provides us with examples. We can do what we know.

Rahab was of questionable character and made no secret of it. She lived in Jericho as the Israelites sought the Promised Land. Joshua sent spies to survey the Jordan River, and the king of Jericho wasn't pleased. Rahab, a Gentile, believed in the Israelite God, and she trusted that He loved her, too. She had a choice to make. Rahab hid and protected the spies (Joshua 2:4). Then she let them escape.

So she let them down by a rope through the window,
for the house she lived in was part of the city wall.
Now she had said to them,
"Go to the hills so the pursuers will not find you.
Hide yourselves there three days until they return,
and then go on your way."

JOSHUA 2:15–16 NIV

Rahab's insight was incredible, and there is no doubt she

overcame great obstacles and prejudices to be true to the mission God prepared for her. Great insight is filled with great courage. And the courage comes when we do what we know.

Jonathan didn't want to believe his father, Saul, was a danger to his beloved friend David. But it was true, and Jonathan had a choice to make. He stayed true to who he was, despite the risk, and did what he knew to save David's life (1 Samuel 20). When David was about to leave Saul's land, he recognized well the love and loyalty his friend displayed.

David got up from the south side of the stone and bowed down
before Jonathan three times, with his face to the ground.
Then they kissed each other and wept together—
but David wept the most. Jonathan said to David,
"Go in peace, for we have sworn friendship with each other
in the name of the LORD, saying,
'The LORD is witness between you and me,
and between your descendants and my descendants forever.'"

1 SAMUEL 20:41–42 NIV

There is no secret to this part of our insight. We know much, much to begin our decision-making process with, every time. The choice to honor what we know is up to us.

THE KNOWLEDGE OF GOD The light on our path burns brightest when we hold on to the most important things we know, before we try to learn anything else. The *knowledge of God* is a powerful knowledge that transcends all indecision. Basic and always true, it guides us with the light that doesn't fade. It is the power of a *personal, present,* and *prepared* God.

- You know a *personal* God. *"Are not two sparrows sold for a copper coin? And not one of them falls to the ground apart from your Father's will. But the very hairs of your head are all numbered. Do not fear therefore; you are of more value than many sparrows"* (Matthew 10:29–31 NKJV).

We are loved by the greatest God. We are made in His image. He has sacrificed His Son for us. How could He ever let us go when He's already paid for our souls? You are special and unique, and His purpose for you is special and unique. I can't talk on the phone and hear someone in the room with me at the same time, but somehow, some miraculous way, the Lord hears you and me when we both cry. He hears your plea at the same time He hears mine, and His response is personal to what we each need. He is completely your God, and He is completely my God. That is what we know.

- You know a *present* God. *"For I am the LORD, I do not change"* (Malachi 3:6 NKJV).

We learn much from the stories of our ancestors. We will probably never see a flood cover the earth or hear the tale of another man captive three days in the belly of a big fish. But that's okay. The lessons are still there, and there are more to come. Our God can use floods or stock market crashes or imprison us in traffic jams for what seem like three days to remind us of His presence.

Our problems today are high-tech and microwaved, but the God who controls all hasn't changed since time began. His grace and His patience and His instruction and His wisdom are all here, still, right now. He is never more than one breath away, a single breath that calls Him close, now and forever. That is what we know.

- You know a *prepared* God. *"For I know the plans I have for you,"* declares the LORD, *"plans to prosper you and not to harm you, plans to give you hope and a future"* (Jeremiah 29:11 NIV).

The ram was caught in the brush to substitute for Isaac (Genesis 22:13). The colt was tied just as Jesus said it would be to carry Him into Jerusalem (Luke 19:30–32). The "great fish" arrived to swallow Jonah (Jonah 1:17). There was water in the desert for the Ethiopian's baptism (Acts 8:36). God always prepares for His children to do what they know. And because those before us did what they knew, their decisions stand today to remind us of our God who is never surprised.

I have no doubt He has done the same for you. Can you remember a time you did what you knew and found something unexpected, though miraculous, waiting for you? The Lord watches our every step, and while He walks with us, He is also a step ahead, preparing. Because He knows our needs and because He will never withhold His help, He prepares our way even when we can't see it. Even when we have only enough insight to carry us an inch, we can trust that God has prepared our way through eternity. That is what we know.

Our *personal, present,* and *prepared* God is also a *presenting* God, giving us gifts to enjoy and explore all our lives. We need never doubt the *knowledge of gifting* He has placed within us. It's meant to be used.

THE KNOWLEDGE OF GIFTING

There are different kinds of gifts, but the same Spirit.
There are different kinds of service, but the same Lord.
There are different kinds of working,
but the same God works all of them in all men.

1 CORINTHIANS 12:4–6 NIV

If we believe in the love and grace of our Lord, we know we have gifts uniquely ours that He has given to us. They are many, and they are special. Nothing is too small to be seen as a gift from God, and when we think of everything we are that way, we see how the knowledge of all our gifts helps give us the insight we need today and every tomorrow to come.

Every time God has poured His grace on us, we've received new gifts. Maybe you know well the gift of compassion or the gift of understanding. Maybe you have the gift of patience because of a trial you can't end. Have you taken the time to recognize all your gifts? Everything you've survived is everything you've gained, and the time is just waiting for you to put it to use. Those tough decisions you face are excellent places to start.

Let your gifts guide you through your dilemmas. Start with these four.

- *The gift of obedience.* To obey might not seem like a gift, but it is when we realize it's a benchmark to guide us in our decisions. Jesus commanded us to love God and love each other (Luke 10:27). That gift of obedience liberates us from much that threatens to harm us, because it makes our path clearer. It's what we know. Like the Samaritan who didn't struggle with his decision (Luke 10:33–35), we can embrace the gift of obedience in a thousand tiny decisions every day. "Jesus told him, 'Go and do likewise'" (Luke 10:37 NIV).

- *The gift of humility.* It's a paradox. Every minute we spend with God invites more of Him into our hearts and homes, and every minute we learn something more. Yet the more we learn about God and ourselves and about managing our lives, the humbler we become in His presence. That gift of humility guides us in our decisions because it puts us in the only place we can truly understand what's happening—at God's knee, ready to accept His guidance and learn something new.

The more we know, the more we know there is more to learn. We can take everything we've learned before and trust God not to abandon us as we follow it, and at the same time, we submit ourselves to Him so that we find the knowledge we're lacking. Our gift of humility prepares the way for God's wisdom to guide us without fail.

- *The gift of correction.* "Whoever heeds correction shows prudence" (Proverbs 15:5 NIV). We rarely think of correction as a gift, do we? But we rarely forget it, either. As God corrects us, He shows us the better, more lighted path. It is a gift we have to learn to accept over and over again because we can be resistant sometimes, wanting to avoid the correction and move on quickly to God's forgiving arms. But that's not the goal—the correction is a blessed gift all its own, just like God's grace.

Yes, He forgives us out of love, but it doesn't stop there. His gift of correction means that He takes the time to show us where we've hurt ourselves so we don't have to do it again, and insight follows. And with that gift, we can face all the decisions before us, doing what we know because of all the times we didn't.

- *The gift of mercy.* "For You, Lord, are good, and ready to forgive, and abundant in mercy to all those who call upon You" (Psalm 86:5 NKJV). Jesus told Peter a story, and we learn much from it today. The merciful king forgave his servant's large debt and canceled it completely. Then the servant had the chance to do the same with someone who owed him, but he refused. He squandered his gift and failed to see its value, to do what he learned. The king reinstated his debt. "This is how my heavenly Father will treat each of you unless you forgive your brother from your heart" (Matthew 18:35 NIV).

  God's mercy is not dependent on the size of our debts, but on our sincerity, repentance, and willingness to grant the same. With great compassion, He lets His mercy rule His heart, and sooner or later, we'll be faced with the same decision the unmerciful servant was. What will we do? Will we take hold of this amazing gift and do what we know with it? Or will we ignore its power to bring us peace? The decision awaits.

And maybe there's a gift you didn't even know you had, just waiting to be used. We'll talk about that great joy next as part of learning what we don't know.

• • • • •

Think again about your dilemma we talked about earlier. Where can you apply your knowledge of *beginning*, of *God*, of *gifting* to it? What do you know and have neglected or forgotten that can help you in your decision? Have you been reluctant or afraid to do what you know? Go to God with those concerns now.

Show me your ways, O LORD, teach me your paths;
guide me in your truth and teach me,
for you are God my Savior,
and my hope is in you all day long.

PSALM 25:4–5 NIV

Chapter 20

Learn What You Don't Know

"Call to Me, and I will answer you, and show you great and mighty things, which you do not know."

JEREMIAH 33:3 NKJV

"It's a great day when you're learning, don't you think?" the Lord asked.

"I'd like to just know everything," I confessed.

"Of course you would. And you do, as you get to know *Me*. The unveiling of new insight is just a part of the path we walk together. You don't want to miss it."

"And I will learn what I don't know?"

"Yes, every decision is the same, remember, and they all build on one another. You'll learn even more than you were hoping for every time; I guarantee it."

"More? I like it when You say more!"

"Yes, and everything you don't know and have to learn gives you more *courage, strength,* and *joy*."

And I just know insight follows. Sounds like a great path. Let's get started.

• • • • •

INSIGHTFUL COURAGE

I will instruct you and teach you in the way you should go;
I will counsel you and watch over you.

PSALM 32:8 NIV

God is so right. As I've struggled over time to learn what I didn't know, I've found the courage that He said comes with the work. Now, I'm the biggest wimp in all the South, but it's not the courage of a daredevil I'm talking about (*brave* is as alien to my vocabulary as *caramelize* and *coriander*). It's the courage to trust answers will come. It's the courage that believes in the certainty of God's control and instruction.

Today, after too many messes to count and blessed with the kindness of a wise and patient Lord, I see all my new problems in a different way. They come to me almost with a blueprint attached, and what I don't understand, I can learn. Nothing is insurmountable, because there is a guaranteed way to find within the struggle a peace that matches who I am. God has taught me that. No problem is a threat. My thoughts and my soul are grounded in this courage God made to fit me. Fear is quickly recognized as a cancer that doesn't belong in my simple life. It is separate and weak, and I can remove it.

God helps me start every decision process with this courage, this unfailing test to choose what is consistent with everything I know. The order brings peace, no matter what decisions others are making or what else is happening around me. It isn't life in a vacuum, but life in victory of my insight over my insecurities.

You can have that same courage, too, the courage to use the insight you have to find the insight you need. This courage deepens with practice, and you can find more in your *questions, answers,* and *actions*.

COURAGEOUS QUESTIONS When Jesus sent His twelve disciples to minister to the Israelites (Matthew 10:5–6), they were the first of their kind. They may have been unsure, even scared. But they held on to what they knew and prepared to learn what they didn't. Did the disciples know how to gather "lost sheep" when Jesus gave the command? No doubt they were divinely inspired, but they lived in their everyday world facing tremendous hardship. And every experience was something new, every day a different challenge. I imagine they had to make critical decisions at every juncture, and I'm sure they did it with the insight we want for ourselves.

"I am sending you out like sheep among wolves.
Therefore be as shrewd as snakes and as innocent as doves."
MATTHEW 10:16 NIV

The Twelve had to assess their situation and respond to others' choices. They had to learn if they would be welcome with their message, and then summon the courage to carry on if they were or if they weren't. I can only imagine the questions going through their minds as they tried to do their work, to learn what they didn't know. We can learn from their example of courage because the more we know, the more prepared we are to make our decisions. Insight isn't hidden at all.

QUESTIONS FOR OURSELVES

- *What do you bring to the problem?* How would you help someone else in your situation? There is much within you already that will guide you in your current dilemma—you just need to reveal it and let it help you. As you face difficult choices, know that everything you are will sustain you as you learn ways to use it. Look for those opportunities in your decision and rely on strengths you've already tested and those just blossoming.

- *What do you hope to gain?* Sometimes we have to make choices because of life situations—you lose a job, and you have to find a new one. But most of the time, we're making a choice because we want to have more peace in our lives. Look at your dilemma and see what your motivation is. What do you need God to teach you in this chapter of your life? Why is this so important to you? Understand what you want from this situation, and you'll learn the next step to take.

- *What have you lost in past decisions?* Look courageously at the times you've been in situations similar to what you're facing now and see what you can learn. What do you wish you had the chance to do over again? What do you want to recover or change, and how can you do that in your next choice? When we take an honest look at our lives and see what's missing because of poor choices we've made, we find the courage to make better choices. We learn what hasn't worked so we can learn what will.

QUESTIONS FOR OTHERS   God speaks to us in a thousand ways, and sometimes He sends others to help us and guide us, to lead us to revelations we're not finding on our own. Between Jerusalem and Gaza, Philip helped the unenlightened Ethiopian. For all his important position in his work—he was in charge of all Queen Candace's treasury—he didn't know what to do, how to follow his faith. He was doing what he knew, reading the book of Isaiah. Philip asked him if he understood. " 'How can I,' he said, 'unless someone explains it to me?' So he invited Philip to come up and sit with him" (Acts 8:31 NIV). The road the teacher and pupil traveled was desert, yet there was water for the new disciple's baptism (Acts 8:36–38). When we learn and want to go on and learn more, God provides for us, too.

Often the examples of insight from people far wiser than we are serve to enlighten and inspire us. Has someone you trust faced a dilemma like yours? How do your friends see you reacting to your situation? What would they do if the choice were theirs?

Gather from reliable sources all the information you can if you're faced with a difficult decision. Then factor it in to your knowledge of who you are and where God is leading you. You can trust He's not leading you anyplace you don't have the courage to travel, and sometimes we discover more of His great courage through our interaction with others. People show up in your life for a reason.

QUESTIONS OF "WHAT IF" These questions can either paralyze us or propel us. We all know the what-if questions that take away our joy and keep us trapped in a world with no peace. We let the what-ifs of everything that can go wrong prevent us from doing what we need to do. But what if we asked ourselves some other questions? What if we looked at everything that could go *right*?

- *What if. . .*you choose to be a good example of God's love? How can you do that with the decision you're facing? How can you follow your Lord's command to love your neighbor with your choice?

- *What if. . .*you choose to claim a new gift God's given you? How will that decision minister to those around you? How will it change your life in a positive way?

- *What if.* . .you choose to leave behind a destructive way of life? What will your courageous choice mean for your future? How will you fill the vast open spot in which God seeks to dwell?

- *What if.* . .you choose a goal the world would never expect you to reach? How will the Lord make Himself available to you as you begin your journey? How will you honor Him with each step?

- *What if.* . .you choose peace for your life no matter what? How will you surrender your plan to God's will today? What will you do to make that same choice over and over again, to claim your peace every time?

- *What if.* . .you choose more of God? What will that mean to your heart as you prepare to make critical decisions? What evil will you allow *more of God* to permanently displace out of your life?

There's no way we can lose the courage God has planned for us. It's all there, and discovering it through questions is an experience to enjoy all on its own. Everything we've learned helps us learn more. We have our history to guide us and our future to inspire us. Every problem shows its blueprint if we'll look. Every *oops* shouts its *ahh* if we'll listen.

COURAGEOUS ANSWERS

"But what about you?" he asked. "Who do you say I am?"
Simon Peter answered,
"You are the Christ, the Son of the living God."
MATTHEW 16:15–16 NIV

Asking the questions we need to help us learn what we don't know takes courage and gives us courage at the same time. We gain a little more insight into our troubles, and we're able to go on, to get a little closer to the insight we need for our choices. We also find great courage in answering God's questions about where we are in our journey with Him. There may be several, but let's concentrate on just two.

God asks, "How does this choice *deepen* our relationship?" When you answer this question, you'll see where your courage is leading you. Is there something new you need to learn about God's plan for you? Could this decision be part of a deeper dimension you want to experience? Which path in front of you will bring more of God into your life?

Every day we grow or we regress. Nothing stays the same. Choose for yourself if you will build a more intimate relationship with God or if you'll let it fade.

God asks, "How does this choice *reflect* our relationship?" Will you use your decision to witness for God? Will you want to hide it, or will you celebrate it as a step in your journey with the Lord? Your life is made up of thousands of little decisions and big ones, too, but they all have one thing in common—how they reflect your heart to the world around you.

As you think about your answer, remember your model for everything. God reflects His devotion and attention to you in all He does. Yes, His insight is flawless and His courage infinite—and as you answer His questions, you tap into that insight and courage and learn what you need to know.

COURAGEOUS ACTION No decision ends with a yes or no from us. There are actions we have to take no matter which choice we make. Some decisions, like career paths or parenthood, require long-term dedication, and we must learn as we go even when we know we've chosen the best way for ourselves. We go forward with faith to do what we learn along the way, to act courageously on all that's within our control. When we "prepare our minds for action" (1 Peter 1:13), we're preparing our hearts for God. And again, more of Him means more courage for our actions. That's what Mordecai and Esther found.

Far more dramatic and dangerous than anything we're likely to face, Mordecai and his adopted daughter, Esther, risked their lives to pursue what they believed was right. Living in Persia and subject to Persian rule, the Jews were at risk from bigoted, power-hungry Haman, a high official in King Xerxes' court. Mordecai recognized the unusual place Esther was in to help.

King Xerxes had chosen Esther to be his queen, and while that sounds grand and influential, Esther actually had little standing or power. Still, she did what she knew to do and found great courage to lead her in new decisions and actions.

> *Then Esther sent this reply to Mordecai:*
> *"Go, gather together all the Jews who are in Susa, and fast for me.*
> *Do not eat or drink for three days, night or day.*
> *I and my maids will fast as you do.*
> *When this is done, I will go to the king,*
> *even though it is against the law. And if I perish, I perish."*
> ESTHER 4:15–16 NIV

Because of Esther's insight and courage, she not only saved herself and her father, but the whole country's Jewish population, as well. Did she know if her actions would work? And how did she choose her timing and approach? I don't know, but she knew her God was leading her and she could learn what she didn't know if she kept her faith in Him.

Haman, who wanted to annihilate an entire race, found himself hanged from the seventy-five-foot gallows he had built for Mordecai. We rarely face a gallows, but we regularly find ourselves in other situations where our spiritual lives depend on what we do, when we have to learn what being a faithful disciple means. Our decisions aren't usually a matter of life and death, but every decision is a matter of walking on faith or walking outside it.

How do we honor God when we're scared and facing great odds? We find our insight one simple action at a time.

We pray, we seek God's guidance, and we prepare a banquet (Esther 5:8). We make our petition, and we tell the truth. All of these acts of courage add up to the answers we need to move us to a place of peace, where we'll walk on our water with nary a stumble, one brave step at a time.

We sometimes face enemies who want to destroy us, or maybe we're just in the path of someone else's misguided ambition. When that happens, we can accept the situation or learn how to change it through our own acts of courage and obedience to God's Word. Like Esther, you can work where you are, with what is within your control, do what you know, and learn the rest as God teaches. With powerful courage and more powerful belief, your destiny will find you, one victory at a time.

• • • • •

Are you afraid to take action on a project, fearful like Peter walking on water with the Lord? Don't be. All you need is a breath of courage, enough to believe He will "hold you up," and then a lifetime full will follow, with all the courage you need to keep learning what you don't know so you can do what God needs. Every decision requiring great insight requires great courage—how fortunate for us we're in no danger of running out of either because God blesses us with abundant amounts over and over. Our focus on Him guarantees His touch on us. If that fact doesn't give you courage, nothing will.

INSIGHTFUL STRENGTH

It is God who arms me with strength and makes my way perfect.
2 SAMUEL 22:33 NIV

As we step out into the unknown with great courage, we find lots of new decisions to make, lots of other places to learn what we don't know. These tests are personal, too, just like your walk on water with your Lord. We'll learn so much about our strength as we live the decisions of our lives. And each one blesses us with more insight, more of God.

STRENGTH OF CHANGE

Do not conform any longer to the pattern of this world,
but be transformed by the renewing of your mind.
Then you will be able to test and approve what
God's will is—his good, pleasing and perfect will.
ROMANS 12:2 NIV

Do you want to change your life? Many of our decisions are about that great question because everything changes our lives for better or worse. And we can choose to make the change for something better every moment. No matter how weak we've been in the past or how many times we've "conformed to the world," God will grant us the strength to transform the life we have now into the one we want.

You can harness the strength of change, to conform not to this world, when you let the Lord teach you as you go. It takes great strength to admit our mistakes, but when we do, we find greater strength in their place. No matter how lost we've been, we can change direction and follow God with a strength that comes only from Him.

STRENGTH OF CONVICTION

> *"Martha, Martha,"* the Lord answered,
> *"you are worried and upset about many things,*
> *but only one thing is needed. Mary has chosen what is better,*
> *and it will not be taken away from her."*
>
> LUKE 10:41–42 NIV

When we're trying to make choices about our lives, it's easy to become distracted by the confusion of all we have to contend with every day. And it's easy to let less important things overtake the more important things. We learn about the strength of our convictions through those choices.

Think about your convictions as you struggle with a decision. What matters most to you—and to what do you feel called? Don't know for sure? Now is the time to find out. Don't look at your decisions as inconvenient pressures, forcing you into hard circumstances. See them as ways to build the life and legacy you want for yourself. We all have convictions we feel in our hearts—sometimes we just let them get pushed aside in the routine of more mundane things. And sometimes when we falter or make a mistake despite our best intentions, we discover a conviction that won't let us go. It becomes a part of who we are to guide us forever after.

That's why tough decisions are to be welcomed, not wished away, why reconstructing our lives after disarming circumstances or misguided choices is a blessing. These decisions bring us back to the basics of what matters and help us find and rely on the strength of our convictions. They help us learn what we didn't know about ourselves and about our lives in this world, whether we'll choose a simple life with God or whether we'll be content to live in the complications. And as we learn what truly matters, we find more insight to guide us through any mess, every mission. On that strength, we can build anything.

STRENGTH OF SURRENDER

As he looked up, Jesus saw the rich putting their gifts into the temple treasury. He also saw a poor widow put in two very small copper coins. "I tell you the truth," he said, "this poor widow has put in more than all the others. All these people gave their gifts out of their wealth; but she out of her poverty put in all she had to live on."

LUKE 21:1–4 NIV

I can imagine the "poor widow" knew she'd have much to learn, yet she did what she knew with great faith. She surrendered her very life to God, because with no money left, she was clearly depending on God to grant her insight about what to do and where to go next. She was one of the weakest people in the town, yet she had a strength the wealthiest citizens didn't. She gave her last two coins freely, with no boasting or fanfare. Her surrender was between her and her God, but Jesus saw and thought it important enough to share the act with His disciples, and with us. Yet the other people of the story make Jesus' point with their actions, too, because it's in them that we see ourselves.

Surrendering to God is not about placing your last dollar in an offering box but about placing whatever you're holding too tightly into God's hands. We all have a few things we're hoarding, and for many of us, it's our imperfections and flawed past and messy present that we don't know how to surrender to Him. Or maybe it's a power you wield over others that makes you feel superior, a power of ego that scams you with false strength. The wealthy men of the story couldn't give much because they were too afraid to trust in God's care. If we face up to God about all the times we've failed, will He leave us, abandon us to our own means? No!

Whatever we keep from God weakens us. When we surrender it to God, He strengthens us so that we can go forward and learn what we didn't know. Fill your offering box with whatever is claiming you and weakening you by forcing you to cling to it. Is it shame, worry, work, hate, addiction? Let it go and see what happens.

INSIGHTFUL JOY

Fan into flame the gift of God.
2 TIMOTHY 1:6 NIV

We've already talked much about using our gifts. And they are never exhausted. God plants just the right seeds we'll need to grow our gifts and abilities and talents and understandings. Then He leads us to places to use them, and we experience the abundant joy of working in harmony with our Creator. Life is good.

Then there are the times we feel lost for a while, not sure how to respond to the challenges before us. So we pray and read God's Word and claim our courage and strength. We fit our gifts into the equation as well as we can, and yet something's lacking. So we keep praying and surrendering our will to the Lord's, and He creates something amazing out of the mess we've made. He kindles in us a new gift, and a new joy is born: "You have put gladness in my heart" (Psalm 4:7 NKJV).

Your new gift may seem small to you, but it's not. No gift from God is small. Priscilla and Aquila discovered the gift of hospitality (1 Corinthians 16:19). Eunice and Lois discovered the gift of "genuine faith" and passed it on to Timothy, their son and grandson (2 Timothy 1:5 NKJV). Perhaps the "busybodies" in Thessalonica discovered the gift of honest works (2 Thessalonians 3:11–12). And perhaps Euodia and Syntyche discovered the gift of resolution and solved their disputes then and later (Philippians 4:2).

Maybe you'll discover the gift of quiet, the joy of listening more and talking less, because your new problem somehow demands it. Or the gift of empathy might find you, the joy of being able to relate to and encourage others who are hurting in a way you understand.

Our whole lives consist of gifts from God, and everything we do for others in this world reflects those gifts. Harnessing their power and applying all we are to our work is a source of profound joy. And insight follows.

Each new gift reminds us again of God's deep care and provision for our lives. We trust—again—that He will allow nothing for which we are not abundantly equipped. Perhaps the time and attention it takes to discover new gifts is His way of being near us in our troubles. So much is required of us in this complicated world, and we must be at our best to meet it. We must take hold of all the power God has instilled in us.

That power manifests itself in all our unique gifts. Discovering them, claiming them, and letting them guide our lives bathes us in unmatched joy. We can respond to our problems with confidence and choose the path that glorifies God with our gifts, every single one. My cross-stitched picture is right. The Lord will join me in handling whatever comes our way, because together we are prepared.

Go to God and talk to Him about the many gifts He has already given you. Thank Him for the opportunity to use your gifts, and ask Him to help you discover more. Listen for Him to reveal what you need to know—look for the tangible events in your life He might be using to display it. And whatever you discover today will guide you now and in times to come.

Yes, we've all found ourselves in one of those "I can't handle this!" messes, when we're up to our eyeballs in confusion and feel about as capable as an ostrich with a laptop. But that's never how God sees us. He sees us as He made us, full of the gifts we need to complete our work, able to learn and direct our lives with His Word.

No matter how big a mess we find ourselves in, we have the power to get out of it, to create or correct whatever we need. It might very well be the power of a new gift we find to guide us in the right direction. Look deep within as you work your way through these kinds of troubles. Solving every "I can't" with "Yes, by the grace and insight of God, I can!" is a joy reserved especially for us easily overwhelmed souls. The joy is an insight into God's own heart, where nothing is impossible and all is well. The gifts He's saving just for when you need them most are present in abundance. Let them in whenever you want.

· · · · ·

Think again about your dilemma we talked about earlier. Do you think God didn't see it coming? Highly unlikely. That's why you'll be blessed with whatever you need. "For we are God's workmanship, created in Christ Jesus to do good works, which God prepared in advance for us to do" (Ephesians 2:10 NIV). If God prepared the work, He prepared your abilities. Learn what you don't know.

· · · · ·

Part 4

Where can you apply your *courageous questions, answers,* and *actions* to your decision?

_____

_____

_____

Where will your strength of *change, conviction,* and *surrender* enter in? What joy is waiting for you to discover it?

_____

_____

_____

Finally, think about how you will find *peace* in your dilemma as we look ahead to our final point.

> *You will keep him in perfect peace,*
> *Whose mind is stayed on You,*
> *Because he trusts in You.*
> ISAIAH 26:3 NKJV

Chapter 21

Seek Peace

Do not be anxious about anything, but in everything,
by prayer and petition, with thanksgiving,
present your requests to God.
And the peace of God, which transcends all understanding,
will guard your hearts and your minds in Christ Jesus.

PHILIPPIANS 4:6–7 NIV

All of our steps for finding the insight we need come together here—because everything must work together to bring us peace or our lives will never be simple, we'll never have order, and we'll miss out on all the abundance God has prepared for us. Only in a state of peace can we grow and thrive. And here's the best part—the peace we crave breathes inside us every minute. God put it there first, before any doubts or worries or complications we added, and it's just up to us to let it live as He intended.

In our state of God-given peace, the complicated world can't touch us, and finding our peace is not the giant mystery we sometimes think it is. It's the most natural thing in the world because it brings us closer to God. It's only two things—more of God and less of everything else. Funny how we've come full circle to this point, isn't it?

Turn from evil and do good; seek peace and pursue it.
PSALM 34:14 NIV

Sometimes we have to learn the hard way. One of the surest ways to know what brings us peace is to know what doesn't. We've all figured that out. When we've failed to do what we know or learn what we didn't, we've battled rejection, fear, guilt, sorrow, and a nasty pile of other ills. Maybe those experiences are just part of a growing disciple's life. We know we can't change what's happened, but from it, we learn well the value of peace in our hearts.

Like the angels with the dragnet, we can "separate the wicked from among the just" (Matthew 13:47–49 NKJV) we bring into our lives. We can choose what will give us peace or what won't. Sometimes we think we have no control over how peaceful our lives are, but we do. Knowing that gives us the insight to seek and find the peace we need.

Sometimes we choose between two situations to come, looking for the one we believe will bring us peace. And sometimes we find ourselves in situations in which we're hurting and hopeless because of previous choices or circumstances. That's when we have to work within the lines already drawn, to do what we can each day to breathe a little peace into our hearts. That may mean saying no in some cases. It may mean withholding our opinions in others, or letting go of things we can't control while holding on to things we can. Whether our range of options is wide or narrow, we can always touch the peace God has waiting for us.

ONE STEP AT A TIME He always guides us to the place of more peace when He possesses us. Our work is one decision at a time, building on what we know, learning as we go. The more we feel the peace of God in our hearts, the more we want it. And He will never steer us away from that, because secure and strong in a state of peace is how we work best, how we move closer to Him. One pure moment of peace sustains us so we can make way for more.

Pursuing that peace begins to color everything we do, and we realize we can't be without it. There is a hurt and a hole in us in its absence and a great joy and power when it becomes like our heartbeat. Complications fade as we structure our lives around the things that bring us peace, and our insight about those things grows daily.

As you learn to know yourself better, you'll know what you need and will allow into your life—forgiveness, understanding, work, goals, worship, education, patience, love—that will bring you peace. And you'll know what you won't allow—envy, resentment, jealousy, dishonesty, fear, worry, doubt, disorder—that would steal your peace away. It's all your choice, always.

A life lived with God in control is the most peaceful life we can have, today and every day. Hey—that's your life and my life, too. That's good to know.

"Do you understand? My peace is yours, living in you when you live in Me," the Lord said.

"I do understand! There's no peace apart from my trust in You."

"Good, because you have a lot to do, remember?"

"That's my line!" I teased Him with a wink. "Yes, my life is full and busy, but also simple and in order when I trust my insight guided by You. You knew it all along, didn't You?"

"It's part of My job. I have a lot to do, too—I have you."

I pouted, and He laughed at me.

"But I'll never go away. My peace will always be yours. The complicated world can never change that. I love you. I'm here."

Ahh. How much simpler could it be?

But I am like an olive tree flourishing in the house of God;
I trust in God's unfailing love for ever and ever.

PSALM 52:8 NIV

Chapter 22

Peace in the Mess— Like a Peanut in a Bathtub

"This is what the LORD says to you: 'Do not be
afraid or discouraged because of this vast army.
For the battle is not yours, but God's.'"

2 CHRONICLES 20:15 NIV

We all know the good times, when living is easy and life is fun. But because life is life, we all know the tough times, too, when living is pained and life is a struggle. We feel like we're tied to the tracks and our problem, whatever it is, is barreling toward us, always just about to run us over. And every day, it hits us, and we have to get up, pick up that trouble as well as we can, and carry it everywhere we go.

Pretty soon our problem is so big we can't see around it. It consumes us. We have to do something. Desperation is surely the mother of restoration.

I can remember a certain one of those "heavier than heaven and earth" problems I had once. It frustrated me to the point of overtaking my every thought and every moment of calm. I was truly at a loss. I tried perhaps the typical approach. "Please! God, make this go away!" I prayed with all due drama and wailing. He said no, with absolutely no wailing or apology. "It's here to stay," He said.

Perfect. Okay, then egotistical logic took over. *If my problem is here to stay, I can fix it,* I decided. I worked hard to make everyone change and accommodate me, to see things my way. It didn't take long to figure out that wouldn't work, either.

So now what? I was clearly failing to manage this mess on my own. So, tired from the battle and the strain of the problem growing bigger by the day, I prayed for a better way to deal with it. Maybe there was more. Maybe I was missing something in my limited view.

Trying to fix the problem wasn't so sad because I failed, but because I tried to do it *without God.* That was the missing link. That was why there was no insight, no wisdom to everything I tried. I failed, and I felt abandoned and alone. I was hurting, and I needed to feel God's control of my life, which was spiraling unstoppable, out of my control.

God had said He was big ("Do I not fill heaven and earth?" Jeremiah 23:24 NKJV) and powerful ("I am the LORD, the God of all mankind. Is anything too hard for me?" Jeremiah 32:27 NIV), and the not-so-subtle side of me said, "Let's find out."

"Okay, let's do," God responded instantly, and He met me in my misery and darkness to guide me to His light.

I imagined my problem as this big, giant, heavy, ugly,

jagged boulder, and I could barely carry it. But I was holding on as tightly as I could because it was my problem to solve. Then I imagined the "bigness" of God—His grace and love and compassion and power and faithfulness and might and wisdom—all together like a beautiful, giant crucible. The cradle formed when He held His hands together, and His heart beat soft and reassuring, steady and strong.

I staggered under my heavy weight to the edge of the crucible. I looked into the vastness of God's power and threw my oversized problem over the edge—into God's hands. And then I had to smile in awe. It was so funny. That massive, oppressive weight I'd been carrying around breathlessly rattled around like a peanut in a bathtub. In God's hands, it was reduced to its real size. And I could never take it back.

Throwing my problem over the edge didn't make it disappear. God had said no about that. And it didn't make it less serious, because the facts didn't change. But it did make it manageable, because I finally relinquished control of it to God, and He's much better at handling such things than I am. He can cradle your problem, too, consume it, and turn it into anything when it's in His hands.

The wisdom that is from above is first pure,
then peaceable, gentle, willing to yield,
full of mercy and good fruits.

JAMES 3:17 NKJV

When I gave my trouble to God, I could go from hurting to healing. With God in control, I could tackle my problem as He instructed. I could seek and understand His teachings, find my insight to do what I knew and learn what I didn't. And I could have peace no matter what happened.

When I saw its true size and importance next to God's love and grace, I knew that I would be able to handle my problem with God's direction and live my life of service to Him untethered. In His heart, I found the courage and strength to carry on, and in His hands, I left my troubles to await His treatment. That was all I needed to know.

• • • • •

Lord, thank You for Your patience with me as I try to find my place in Your world. I want always to choose the path You would choose for me. I need to feel Your peace in my heart when I drop my life in Your hands and trust Your wisdom. Thank You for my heart's insight that continually leads me to You. Amen.

• • • • •

My Daily Affirmation of Insight

My insight cannot fail when I am true to God and true to me.

Part 5

52 Thoughts on a
More Abundant Life

*"I have come that they may have life,
and that they may have it more abundantly."*

JOHN 10:10 NKJV

"Lord, please grant me an abundant life."
"Beloved, I already have."

That's what we all want, isn't it? We want an abundant life in our Lord, full of simplicity, order, and insight. Okay, we can have it, He says, if we follow Him. The "they" Jesus speaks of in John 10:10 are the followers who answer to their Shepherd, the One who calls them "His own" because *He possesses them.* The followers' abundance is tied up in that relationship, and keeping that relationship for myself becomes a goal.

I'm not a perfect disciple now and never will be, but I will always have more of a peaceful and abundant life when I make every choice part of that goal. And because the Lord never abandons but always chooses to bless abundantly with His grace and guidance, I can do that more easily every day. He allows for my many imperfections. He has shown me how everything I do, even a mistake or a complication, is a way to reach out to Him, to beckon more of Him and His peace into my heart.

"Every day is another chance, another choice," the Lord said.

"Yeah, another chance for me to mess up. Have You noticed how I do that so well?"

"Don't think like that. Look how far you've come! Look how much simpler things are now than just a short time ago. And there is always more."

"More messes?"

"Well, probably, but don't worry about it." He smiled at me. "I mean more of Me, remember? I'm like a perpetual calendar—you'll never get to the end of My abundance."

"*You're* prepared and ready. What do *I* do?"

"You cherish the journey. I'll meet you everywhere."

With that reminder of the Lord's infinity of grace and love, I could see that time means nothing. Our lives mean so much more when measured by the heart instead of by the clock, but if we need a way to monitor our progress, the real-life calendar we have will do as well as anything. The Lord meets us in the everydayness because it's moment by moment and miracle by miracle that we learn, no matter how far back we start.

ONE DAY AT A TIME We didn't lose hold of God's abundance in a day or a week. We didn't create our clutter and disorder in a flash, and we didn't get lost overnight. Getting where we *don't* want to be took time, and getting where we *do* want to be will take time, too. That thought would be depressing if we had to make the journey alone. But we don't. As long as we're keeping our feet on the path, thinking one more God-centered thought a day, breathing one more breath of His power each moment, we'll feel Him with us in this quest to simplify our lives.

"Take your time; don't miss a thing," He told me.

"Is everything a lesson?"

"It has to be, in your case," He said, but the closeness of His heart let me know He loves me anyway.

I think the point the Lord was trying, oh so indelicately, to make is that we have to live in our finite, human world. We cannot ascend to mountaintops or travel through time to create the peaceful life we want. Our abundance lives for us in a way we can feel it and see it. It's not some uncatchable wisp of a dream or imagination.

If we choose, we'll find it through every amazing, everyday experience, and just like He said, the simplicity, order, and insight we need will *find us*. Nothing is hidden, and the discovery of it is the miracle of our everyday walk. Our willingness to journey makes it possible. God's abundance makes it spectacular. It's a cherished trip, indeed.

> *This is the day the LORD has made;*
> *let us rejoice and be glad in it.*
> PSALM 118:24 NIV

· · · · ·

I hope you'll use the final part of this book to supplement your daily prayers and readings. Give yourself time to build the life you and God want. Expect great challenges and revelations; take hold of your opportunities and awakenings. The Lord will respond whenever you ask, and you'll discover abundance wherever you look. Remember, there's no end.

In these 52 Thoughts, you'll find one point to reflect on each week of the year. But nothing stays the same. You'll meet new situations every day, welcome new people into your life, encounter absence and loss, challenge and discovery. So after you finish the list this year, you may want to start it over again next year, when a thought will perhaps speak to you in a new way or God will use a new circumstance to bless you with more purpose, grace, and security. And I know you'll have your own thoughts to add, as well.

You will find your abundant life when you choose to. God has already planned it. The peace is there in every complication when you look for more before less—more of God, first and always. I pray our weekly thoughts will help you on your journey.

Mercy, peace and love be yours in abundance.
JUDE 2 NIV

Week 1
An Abundance of Work

All Scripture is given by inspiration of God,
and is profitable for doctrine, for reproof,
for correction, for instruction in righteousness,
that the man of God may be complete,
thoroughly equipped for every good work.

2 TIMOTHY 3:16–17 NKJV

I've been writing this book as my son finishes high school and prepares to leave for college. We've labored to complete more renovations to our house. A hot southern summer has refused to relinquish its grip on my needy garden. I even forgot my own birthday. Could I have planned things any worse? Probably not. My timing for this work has meant full days and short nights, and it has required the focus of a surgeon's laser. Still, it is an *abundance of work* for which I am grateful.

Things are busy, yes, but not complicated. Choices of what to do with my waking hours are easy to make. Goals abound. Perhaps you know the feeling of work that's a mission. Everything I've done during this busy time has been part of every greater mission I have. I'm breathing in my water, and all is well.

When have you experienced an *abundance of work*? Did you feel blessed and busy, or did it complicate things? How can you start with *more* before *less* the next time work consumes you? What blessings have you received from your *abundance of work*, and what work is waiting for you this week?

Week 2
An Abundance of Now

For we brought nothing into this world,
and it is certain we can carry nothing out.

1 TIMOTHY 6:7 NKJV

We don't know what tomorrow will bring, or if it'll come at all. Sure, we make plans and set goals, start diets and plant seeds, take out a mortgage and save for retirement (okay, so maybe I'll get to that one tomorrow). The point is that we have to live like we know tomorrow will come, because for most of us, it will. Living with an *abundance of now*, though, makes today the best it can be.

There's a difference between planning and obsessing. Planning for tomorrow doesn't mean abandoning the joy of today. And that joy begins in the fullness of Christ. When we walk with Him each day, the life on this side of death is the same as the other. We have what we need the most when we begin with our faith. We came here without the knowledge of a personal relationship with our Savior, but when we discovered it, everything changed. That deep, abiding, pervasive connection turned now into the most important moment of our lives. When we let it guide us, we have a joy no disturbance of time or place can overtake.

How are you living your *abundance of now*? Do you sometimes fall into an obsession about tomorrow and forget about the glory of today? Live this week responsibly, planning for the future you're building, and at the same time, claim now for the intimate joy your Father wants to share with you.

Week 3
An Abundance of Health

While Jesus was having dinner at Matthew's house, many tax collectors and "sinners" came and ate with him and his disciples. When the Pharisees saw this, they asked his disciples, "Why does your teacher eat with tax collectors and 'sinners'?" On hearing this, Jesus said, "It is not the healthy who need a doctor, but the sick."

MATTHEW 9:10–12 NIV

How comforting to know that the Lord isn't afraid to dine with us sinners! He doesn't shy away from us or wait until we're more pleasing to meet us. That's why He came to live and die for us—not because we're perfect, but because we're *not*. And in our state of sickness, we find an *abundance of health* promised by God.

Our bodies are weak, and colds and cancers take hold of us. We need a doctor. Our spirits are weak sometimes, too, and sorrows and sadness take hold of us. We need a God who isn't afraid of anything that ails us. We can only become well when the love and grace of the Lord touches us. And He stands ready, always attentive to our needs, even if others watch and wonder if He's making a mistake to love us still, when we look anything but lovable.

Do you feel safe going to God, sick and in pain, looking for your *abundance of health*? Will you let Him work His healing power on your heart, or do you want to heal yourself? Chicken soup may cure a lot of ills, but the sick soul is far more serious than the sick body. There's only one way to true health, and God meets us where we are to grant it. How will you meet Him this week and open your ailing heart to His healing one?

Week 4
An Abundance of Freedom

But now that you have been set free from sin
and have become slaves to God,
the benefit you reap leads to holiness,
and the result is eternal life.

ROMANS 6:22 NIV

We all want to be free, and when we abandon the slavery we've imposed upon ourselves, we prepare the way for a new life. We may have let ourselves become slaves to anything from greed to ego to fear. But we don't have to remain in that state of captivity. We can choose to leave it behind and belong to God. We can embrace our *abundance of freedom*, our gift to be who we were created to be in God's great plan.

Becoming "slaves to God," as Paul says, is not the oppression that slavery to this world is. Belonging to God is the only way we can be free—free from the entanglements of this world so we can live our lives in the peaceful confidence and security of His love. When we're free in God's plan, we know we'll be loved by Him through anything that happens, guided by His grace through every step we take. It's a slavery we choose because the Master calls us His own.

Have you ever lost sight of the freedom belonging to God gives? Sometimes we forget what awaits us when we give our lives to Him, the great adventure and purpose we'll only touch when we are His. Reclaim your *abundance of freedom* this week and revel in the joy of being one of God's own.

Week 5
An Abundance of Integrity

*The man of integrity walks securely, but he
who takes crooked paths will be found out.*

PROVERBS 10:9 NIV

Years and years and years and years ago (in pre-bifocal
days), I was a newspaper reporter. One assignment was to
interview the new local postmaster (no major metropolis,
understand, so that really was news). Anyway, when I called
him to schedule an appointment, he said he didn't want to
see me, that he didn't trust reporters. But it was sort of small-
town tradition that he comply with the paper's request, and
soon we were face-to-face. I tried to reassure him I'd only
write what he told me, but he'd just smirk and say, "Sure, you
will." I checked my spelling and double-checked my notes
and wrote the story. It was my job.

A couple days later, the story took its place on the front
page of the feature section. I couldn't see anything wrong
with it, but I feared Mr. Postmaster would, given his fond-
ness for reporters. I held my breath when I answered my
phone and heard him on the other end. "I just wanted to call
and say thanks. You wrote what I told you," he said. I won-
dered why he sounded so surprised. I could misrepresent his
story no easier than I could my own. Whether he believed
me or not, I had to pursue the *abundance of integrity* that
guides us in those everyday encounters, the prevailing sense
of honor and duty that won't steer us wrong. God responds
to us with the same *abundance of integrity*. He never fails to
hold up His end of the equation.

The postmaster's call was a bonus, but the real payoff

came when I turned in the story. I knew it was true even though I could have made it false. We always have the choice of integrity or something less, regardless of others' beliefs. Have you experienced someone questioning your integrity? How did you respond? How do you work to keep your *abundance of integrity* in every situation?

Week 6
An Abundance of Aim

Aim for perfection, listen to my appeal,
be of one mind, live in peace.
And the God of love and peace will be with you.

2 CORINTHIANS 13:11 NIV

We all know what it's like to get kicked in the teeth by others, or to do it to ourselves. We know well the agony of defeat after defeat, the horrible feelings of inferiority when we can't seem to do anything right. Paul must have known we'd have those days (and weeks—years, even), so he encouraged us to keep an *abundance of aim.* If we can remember the journey always continues, we can forgive ourselves the errant detour, recover from the occasional pothole. The aim is for perfection; the walk is with God.

When we do our best, it's always good enough where it counts. We might not win the prize or set the record, but if we've stretched with all our hearts and held nothing back from our effort, that's perfect enough for God. He knows we'll fail from time to time, but He expects we'll do our best every time. Yes, the walk is tough now and then, but the Guide never changes. And for that reason, we can get back on track when we've strayed and know that our aim for perfection remains.

Are you striving for something right now? Have you lost your *abundance of aim,* being content to drift away from the great bounty God has prepared for you? Regain it this week. Forget your failures and spend some time thinking about an area or two where you're missing the joy of effort and service. Name just a few ways you'll regain your *abundance of aim*.

Week 7
An Abundance of Preface

"I will return again to you, God willing."
ACTS 18:21 NKJV

The Jews of Ephesus asked Paul to remain with them awhile longer, but he told them he had to go to Jerusalem. He promised to return if it was God's will. He prefaced his vow with God's sovereignty. Was he trying to avoid responsibility or dodge their question? No. When we say "God willing" today, are we clinging to His omnipotence or our own wishes? I believe Paul answered their plea the way he did as a reminder of who holds us and the whole world in His hands.

When we preface our plans and our decisions and our work with God's will, we open our spirits up to His. It's not an abandonment of effort and conviction, but rather a practice we turn into a partnership. Then we can better hear the Lord's guidance and direction. We permit ourselves to work where we are, to make ourselves available to a will far superior to our own. When we hold on to an *abundance of preface*, we remind ourselves we can always choose to follow the leanings of a Lord who will never lead us astray.

How have you prefaced your plans lately? Have you gone to God first, listened for His instruction, sought His counsel? It's easy to get wrapped up in deadlines and to-do lists, to hurry through life and sometimes find ourselves in the wrong place. Think about your *abundance of preface* this week and see how you can apply it to some specific areas of your life. Go ahead, it's a partnership you don't want to miss.

Week 8
An Abundance of Example

*"I have set you an example
that you should do as I have done for you."*

JOHN 13:15 NIV

When Jesus washed Peter's feet, He showed him and us more than a custom of the time. He demonstrated for us the servant's heart we need in our walk in this world. In all our efforts to achieve and accomplish, we sometimes forget the basic call to serve one another in love. If we lose our connection with those around us, all we do becomes empty and void. But it doesn't have to be that way. We can look for the *abundance of example* the Lord gave us and find ways to exercise our own each day.

Each action we take affects someone else in some way, and we decide how. It's up to us to serve in His name and become an example to those around us. And we do that best by keeping it simple, because serving doesn't have to mean giving life and limb. It also means reaching out with understanding and acceptance, touching others with grace and compassion, teaching others with humility and patience. We're mistaken to think we can only demonstrate God's love in grand ways. Each interaction with a friend or a stranger is a grand opportunity, a blessed way to be like Jesus, every day.

How do you share your *abundance of example*? Have you missed or ignored an opportunity because you thought it wasn't "important" or "valuable" enough? Pay attention this week and see how you can be a grand example in even the smallest of ways. Nothing is unimportant when it demonstrates the love of God.

Week 9
An Abundance of Forgetfulness

Remember not the sins of my youth and my rebellious ways;
according to your love remember me, for you are good, O LORD.

PSALM 25:7 NIV

When I had to be out of town on garbage day, I pointed out the importance of this weekly event to my husband. I arrived home the next day and saw the can sitting in its rightful place. Hmm, he remembered to put the garbage out and bring the can back, too? Uh, no. Not only was a week's worth of garbage in there, but so was the cat's latest feathered conquest.

"Didn't you see my note about the garbage?"

"Oh. . .I forgot to read it."

I guess I shouldn't complain. My husband also loses count of how many vacuum cleaners I've destroyed and kindly forgets how lumpy my gravy is most of the time. It doesn't matter to him.

Our Lord has a similar approach. He gives us a new start every day, a chance to make things better when we ask. He forgets our shortcomings and concentrates on our work *today*, our walk *today* to follow where He leads. He loses count of our failures and kindly forgets our imperfections. It doesn't matter to Him.

We can be grateful for the Lord's *abundance of forgetfulness*, and we can practice it ourselves. We can keep our focus on the road ahead and avoid the distraction the "broken vacuum cleaners" of the past can be. How will you practice your *abundance of forgetfulness* for yourself and for others? What are you holding on to that you can choose to forget this week? Feel the weight lifted from your heart when you do.

Week 10
An Abundance of Awakening

Jesus said to them, "Loose him, and let him go."

JOHN 11:44 NKJV

Jesus brought Lazarus back into the living world and sent him on his way. That's what He does for us when He "awakens" us. He brings us to life, removes everything that binds us, and sends us on our way. Do you know that feeling when you've been spiritually dead and then the Lord removes the grave clothes that were holding you down? Do you know the feeling when you've been released and restored, when you've been made alive and free?

We need only go to God with whatever is "killing" us, and He will help us loosen its grip. We'll still have the troubles of a flesh-and-blood world, but we don't have to face them from the disadvantage of a grave. We can cry to Jesus and hear Him respond. And when He does, we are free to go. We are free to leave the empty tomb of our failures or oppressions and follow wherever He leads. There is too much wonder in store for us to turn down His *abundance of awakening* for our hearts!

I can only imagine how Lazarus must have felt when he was no longer dead. I know how I've felt when the living God has moved into my heart and shown me how to breathe in His grace. I know you know, too. Nothing can outlive that. Ask God to release you from whatever is holding you down and "dead." Ask Him this week to breathe His *abundance of awakening* on you. Ask Him to direct your steps and use your reawakened soul for only His great purpose.

Week 11
An Abundance of Talents

" 'Well done, good and faithful servant!
You have been faithful with a few things;
I will put you in charge of many things.
Come and share your master's happiness!' "

MATTHEW 25:21 NIV

In Jesus' parable, the master rewarded his servants who were faithful with the money they were given for the test. They wanted to demonstrate their devotion, and their acts of service brought them blessings they couldn't have manufactured on their own. Their faithfulness changed their lives. The result is true for us today, because nothing stays the same.

Our "talents," not of money but abilities, are not meant to be stagnant, guarded. Only when we put them to use can they grow, and then look what happens: We find more! God has given us an *abundance of talents*, an abundance of His touch on our lives that just keeps manifesting itself. Every seed we plant, every heart we help is a talent we refuse to bury. And we'll keep finding more seeds and hearts as long as we look. Our "charge" will increase to fit our talents. It's God's plan and promise.

What are you doing with your *abundance of talents*? Is your faithfulness guiding you, or is your fear? The Lord never gave you anything to hide, so don't be afraid. Think about your *abundance of talents* this week. How can you grow your talents and use them to demonstrate your devotion to the Giver?

Week 12
An Abundance of Refreshing

"Repent, then, and turn to God,
so that your sins may be wiped out,
that times of refreshing may come from the Lord."

ACTS 3:19 NIV

After Peter healed the crippled man at the temple gate called Beautiful (Acts 3:1–10), the people who witnessed the man's health and joy were amazed. They followed Peter, and he told them how the man was made well through his faith in Jesus. Peter promised an *abundance of refreshing* waiting for them, too, when they chose to follow Christ. The time is always right for turning to God.

Peter made his point clearly. God forgives when we repent. And what follows is a healing for our souls far greater than any physical gains. Perhaps you've felt the Lord's *abundance of refreshing* when you've gone to Him, heart to heart, and rested in His mercy. Maybe you can remember the last time you knew the joy the healed man must have felt as he was "walking and jumping, and praising God" (Acts 3:8 NIV). There is no refreshment like that of God, that deep touch that makes all things new.

Don't be afraid to "turn to God" with anything that's broken. He will make it right. He will meet you with an *abundance of refreshing* when you ask. Enjoy this week in God's restorative power. Go to Him now and know the refreshing your soul craves.

Week 13
An Abundance of Acceptance

May the God who gives endurance and encouragement give you
a spirit of unity among yourselves as you follow Christ Jesus,
so that with one heart and mouth you may glorify
the God and Father of our Lord Jesus Christ.
Accept one another, then, just as Christ accepted you,
in order to bring praise to God.

ROMANS 15:5–7 NIV

I do radio interviews by phone every now and then, and they're rarely in my southern backyard. One day, after listeners and hosts in Washington, D.C., could no longer hear me, but before the station disconnected my line, I could hear my hosts commenting on this hint of an accent I have. They weren't cruel at all, and I just smiled as they talked.

I can't hear the drawl myself, but I know they're right, just like all the others have been. But they, and I, have accepted this quirk of my birthplace, and it doesn't get in the way of our message, so I don't worry too much about it. I can use the *abundance of acceptance* God has given me for myself in this case, and for others, too, in lots of cases. I can accept others' flaws with kindness and not worry too much about them. For them and me, I can move on to greater things that need my attention.

When we meet the world around us, and ourselves, with a little more acceptance, we open our eyes to what comes next. Our goals are still waiting; our work remains. And who sets this example for us best of all besides our Lord? His *abundance of acceptance* for us is immense, forever. He doesn't even mind a little accent.

What have you been reluctant to accept about yourself or others? Why? Claim your *abundance of acceptance* this week and put some things in order in your life. Don't let that which you can accept get between you and the enjoyment and purpose of your life. Get back to your goals.

Week 14
An Abundance of Willingness

A man with leprosy came to him and begged him on his knees,
"If you are willing, you can make me clean."
Filled with compassion, Jesus reached out his hand
and touched the man. "I am willing," he said. "Be clean!"

MARK 1:40–41 NIV

Jesus could do anything He wanted—or refuse it. Something in the leper's plea touched His heart, though, and He responded with an *abundance of willingness*. It's the same way He responds to us when we, too, are begging on our knees. Jesus let His compassion overrule the law against touching lepers. Perhaps He sometimes lets His compassion overrule the better judgment it might be to ignore *my* pleas, but that's another story. . . . The consistency of our Lord's willingness to answer us is unwavering.

His *abundance of willingness* to run to us moves all obstacles out of the way. In your moment of pain, there is only you and Him. If He is willing, He can make you whole. And what do you think the chances are that He won't be willing? Absolutely zero. It's our *abundance of willingness* to *ask* that activates His *abundance of willingness* to *give*. Have you asked lately?

Have you approached your Lord with faith and love and asked for His help? Have you counted on His willingness to respond, to touch you, to make you whole? Don't doubt. Don't wait out of fear or shame. Be willing to go to Him this week and accept His *abundance of willingness* to respond.

Week 15
An Abundance of Perseverance

"But the seed on good soil
stands for those with a noble and good heart,
who hear the word, retain it, and by persevering produce a crop."

LUKE 8:15 NIV

Jesus told the story of the seeds that die and the seeds that live. Our lives are full of the seeds of God's Word that we will grow or not. They fall upon us and wait for our response. God's Word never changes. Always, He is leading us toward the more peaceful place. What is yet to be seen is our application of it, of how we will hold on to the Lord's Word through everything contrary to it and use it in our lives. Will we claim our *abundance of perseverance* and withstand all that the complicated world throws at us? Or will we let the seeds die and lose the knowledge and security of God's wisdom?

We have to make that choice because the seeds are ours, God's plan for us to produce the crop only we can. We have to persevere through the devil's assaults, tests and trials, temptations and aggravations of all kinds, but the seeds are still the same. God's Word is still the same. Holding on to it or letting it go is the life or death of our calling. Yes, we'll have to work through many complications, but the crop that follows if we do will make all the toil worthwhile.

Have you let your *abundance of perseverance* become influenced by the ways of the world lately? Have you missed a bounty because you gave up too easily? Think about ways to persevere this week in areas difficult for you. Read God's Word on the subject and plant even more seeds of His love and guidance.

Week 16
An Abundance of Solitude

But Jesus often withdrew to lonely places and prayed.

LUKE 5:16 NIV

Perhaps your life is like mine, and you, too, often need lonely places to withdraw and be quiet. I think we read of Jesus needing to be alone so we'll know the feeling is natural and even welcomed by our Father. Like Jesus, we need an *abundance of solitude*, time away from others just to pray.

You probably know how high your stress level rises when you've had no time to yourself. God feels it, too. He desires intimate time with you, time to talk, time to listen. If we fill our waking hours with too much clutter, we lose touch with the simple relationship we have with God, the relationship of Father and child. He is always there, so glad you've come to be with Him alone when you could have chosen something else.

But how do we find the solitude we need with this busy life and overcrowded schedule? How do we give ourselves permission to retreat? Perhaps the better question is: *How do we not?* We don't have to neglect our families or jobs to find the solitude we need. There is an *abundance of solitude* when we let the Lord show us where it is. Listen for His cries to you. Feel in your heart when He's calling you close. Take the time and space you need—just a few moments will be enough sometimes—to reaffirm His love and presence. Just a bit of sacred solitude will refresh and renew you in ways that work and worry never can. Learn to be quiet, to be still, to spend time with your Father when He calls. He can speak a lifetime in a breath.

Will you listen for God to call you this week? Choose to claim your *abundance of solitude* and rest in His closeness. Pray to Him and hear Him answer you. You'll come to value this practice as much as Jesus did. There is great solace in the solitude.

Week 17
An Abundance of Anchor

We have this hope as an anchor for the soul, firm and secure.

HEBREWS 6:19 NIV

I hang my laundry on the line every day it doesn't rain. It takes longer than throwing the clothes in the dryer, but I like it. One day, I didn't like it. I had the whole line full, like most days. Just as I reached to untie my clothespin apron, I heard a strange sound, like a cork being pulled out of a wooden bottle. In three seconds, all of my clean clothes were on the still-wet ground in the beautiful morning sun that was going to waste. I took a deep breath, unpinned everything, and lugged the heavy basket back inside.

The line had come loose from the corner of the house. When my husband put it back up, he said he anchored it well, so that even I shouldn't be able to break it. The line broke because the weight on it was too great for its supports. There was no *abundance of anchor* to sustain the strain. That never happens with God. He never snaps under the weight of anything we give Him. He holds us taut and straight when we lean on Him. Sometimes He sends others to help us with the load. Can you remember a time someone held you up through your pain? I know you've been an anchor for others, too.

Look around this week and see where God has placed your *abundance of anchor* and where the opportunities are for you to be part of the abundance. Give Him something heavy and see what happens. My clothesline is strong and secure now. And my anchor of God will never loosen. How does yours feel?

Week 18
An Abundance of Following

"When he has brought out all his own, he goes on ahead of them, and his sheep follow him because they know his voice. My sheep listen to my voice; I know them, and they follow me."

JOHN 10:4, 27 NIV

If your sense of direction is so bad you get lost in a phone booth, don't worry. It's not a good sense of direction we need to navigate this world—only the knowledge of where to take the next step. Jesus said sheep always know their next step because they follow their shepherd, and we can follow ours when we know His voice. The shepherd calls his sheep "by name," and Jesus calls us the same way. That relationship is all we need to know. His voice is there to love us and protect us from the world that calls us elsewhere.

When we exercise our *abundance of following*, we're keeping our eyes on our Lord and going where He leads. It's not complicated or scary, but comforting and powerful instead. The shepherd will only lead his sheep where he wants them to go. Our Shepherd does the same.

If you've lost your *abundance of following*, maybe it's because of all the noise of this world in your heart— drowning out your Shepherd's voice. Be still and listen. Reconnect this week to the relationship you and your Father have. Let it grow and become *more* as He leads you safely where you need to go.

Week 19
An Abundance of Choice

"If you do what is right, will you not be accepted?
But if you do not do what is right,
sin is crouching at your door; it desires to have you,
but you must master it."

GENESIS 4:7 NIV

We've talked a lot about choice in our book, and that's because it's a common thread through everything in our lives. When our *attitude* doesn't match our *actions*, something always goes wrong. Every action is a choice, and it's up to us to make it simple or complicated, to bring more peace to our lives or less, to let it reflect our truth or to not. Cain's sacrifice of "fruits of the soil" was not flawed, but his attitude was. And the Lord lays that choice squarely on Cain's shoulders. He does the same with us today. We have an *abundance of choice* in everything we do, and it starts with our devotion to God.

The complicated world lives to pull us away from our devotion, to make our choices hard and stressful, but we can master it if we stay true to our beliefs. We can make every choice difficult, or we can make them all simple. The key is in remembering that our choices are always *ours*. The responsibility is God-given, and mastering the elements that threaten to steal our peace is one of life's great blessings.

How are you exercising your *abundance of choice*? Are you letting someone else choose for you, falling victim to another's influence, or sacrificing fruits without real devotion? It's all your call. Take back your *abundance of choice* today and give it a great workout this week. You'll be amazed at how good it feels.

Week 20
An Abundance of Fruit

"Then he said to the keeper of his vineyard,
'Look, for three years I have come seeking fruit
on this fig tree and find none.
Cut it down; why does it use up the ground?'
But he answered and said to him,
'Sir, let it alone this year also,
until I dig around it and fertilize it.
And if it bears fruit, well.
But if not, after that you can cut it down.'"

LUKE 13:7–9 NKJV

Well, we've all been the barren fig tree a few times, haven't we? Or maybe it's just me, but I know God never gives up on us. If we accept His tending, we can leave our barren years in the past and bear an *abundance of fruit* where we've had none before. And what joy that is! Your fruit may be Nobel prizes or noble acts of simple kindness. It doesn't matter. When you let the Lord garden in your heart, good things grow.

If you've rejected or disallowed your fruit, find out why. Do you feel incapable or unworthy? Nonsense. Do you feel fruitless? God didn't make you that way. We each have seeds of greatness, but they don't burst from the soil of our hearts by themselves. They need our willingness and God's touch. When we allow Him in to "dig and fertilize," we permit the growth of our gifts. Like each fig and fig tree, your fruit can only come from you, and any barrenness in the past is irrelevant. The sun shines on your growth *today*.

Will you invite the Lord in to garden in your heart? How about this week? Thank Him for your *abundance of fruit* and waste no more time in beginning your harvest.

Week 21
An Abundance of Ministry

As each one has received a gift, minister it to one another,
as good stewards of the manifold grace of God.

1 PETER 4:10 NKJV

When I began to write my books of discovery of God, writing was just between Him and me. Every word was a step in my pursuit of Him, every subject something I had lived. That part of my writing hasn't changed, but today thousands of people join me on this continuing journey.

Some of them call my work my ministry. I never thought of it that way. It's a ministry, that's true, but it's God's ministry to *me*, an *abundance of ministry* where the need is truly great. He endures all my lapses to bring me to the learning. He takes every hurt and turns it into hope. He does it all for me, and then He says there's more, and that's where you, my reader, come in. We find each other as He designed.

I know He's doing the same for you in *your* ministry, in how He's ministering to you right now. Every *abundance of ministry* begins where you are and grows with the nourishing grace of God. How will you share yours this week and beyond?

Week 22
An Abundance of Perspective

"Yours, O LORD, is the greatness
and the power and the glory and the majesty
and the splendor, for everything in heaven and earth is yours."

1 CHRONICLES 29:11 NIV

It never fails. In every war film, a character says something about how war makes you see what really matters. In a time of destruction and disorder, hunger and hopelessness, thoughts of greed and pettiness and self-importance fall victim to just surviving. Sharing food or providing sanctuary are far more likely than arguments or ego. But absent a war zone, every day we complain about things so irrelevant. We ignore others' needs to protect our feelings. We lose sight of our goals to prove a point.

God never loses His *abundance of perspective*, no matter how often we do. He always knows what's truly important and proves it by His faithfulness. Your repentance is more important than your regressions, your faith more important than your failures, your future more important than your past. He always sees what truly matters.

Can you see any places where you've lost your perspective lately? Maybe you've forgotten just how much God wants you with Him, how much your attention means to Him. And what does the big picture of your life look like? Would wartime change your perspective? How can you start this week to restore an *abundance of perspective* to your life?

Week 23
An Abundance of Prayer

Now it came to pass in those days that
He went out to the mountain to pray,
and continued all night in prayer to God.

LUKE 6:12 NKJV

The night before Jesus chose His twelve apostles, He spent it alone, praying to God. What joy that must have been for both of them! We are blessed with our own *abundance of prayer*, God's personal invitation to us to meet with Him alone. Sometimes praying is all we can do for a situation, and when we do, that's enough.

Prayer is not a prepackaged or measured commodity. It's a mobile, working, dynamic interaction with our Father. When we pray, He listens. When we listen, He responds. If we limit our prayers to specific times or places, we miss out on one of the warmest parts of our relationship with God. I love to know He's there when I pray in the morning and when I pray in the night, when I see His work and stop to talk to Him about it right then, when I need His immediate guidance and want to hear His voice, when I'm reminded of His control and stop to rest in His arms. Our *abundance of prayer* is our abundance of peace.

Look at each day this week as a special opportunity to interact with your Lord. Meet Him in unlikely places, and invite Him through every door of your heart. Claim your *abundance of prayer*, talk, listen, rest. God is waiting.

Week 24
An Abundance of Light

"I am the light of the world.
He who follows Me shall not walk in darkness,
but have the light of life."

JOHN 8:12 NKJV

Do you ever flip on the light switch even when the power is off, out of habit? We become quite dependent on our electrical power, and it's an inconvenience when we don't have it. We can't do anything we want to do. But it passes. Without the power of God in our lives, however, we are helpless. It's like trying to navigate in a black hole with nothing to guide us. But if we follow the *abundance of light* our Lord provides, we can see. And more than that, we can feel.

Our world is dark sometimes, when we've cut the power ourselves or when others have shut us out. Following Him is the answer to the darkness, Jesus tells us. And how do we do that? How do we reignite the power within our souls? We claim the *abundance of light* that outshines all. We ask Him to touch everything and guide us, one illuminated step at a time, and we feel the warmth of His light as soon as we ask.

Have you felt in the dark before, as if the power were cut to your strength and happiness? Why? Did you refuse to follow the Lord, or did someone lead you astray? It doesn't matter. Your *abundance of light* remains, ever ready to guide you and hold you. Make a step out of the darkness this week and into the power of God. See how it feels. Chances are you'll want to stay in His light.

Week 25
An Abundance of Kindness

An anxious heart weighs a man down,
but a kind word cheers him up.

PROVERBS 12:25 NIV

I was unloading my overflowing cart at the grocery store the other day when a young woman took her place in line behind me. She had a couple of items. "You can go ahead," I told her and motioned to the empty spot on the conveyor belt ahead of the half of the store I had selected.

She looked dead at me without taking a step. "Are you sure? Thank you! No one's ever done that for me before," she said in almost a whisper.

"No problem," I said. *No one had ever done that for her before?* On the one occasion a year when I get to shop for only a couple items, someone always does it for me. She, though, seemed genuinely surprised.

As she finished paying, I was still digging boxes and cans out of my cart. But she got my attention. "Thank you again," she said and smiled. It was such a little thing to me, but to her, that day, it was an *abundance of kindness* from a stranger. I hope I've been as appreciative as she was when others have reached out with their kindness to me. And I hope I never miss the opportunity to tap the *abundance of kindness* the Lord has given me so that I can share it with those around me.

Can you think of some times when someone's unexpected kindness touched your heart? When have you been able to share yours with others? Take notice this week of at least one opportunity to surprise someone with an *abundance of kindness*. And be grateful for those who surprise you!

Week 26
An Abundance of Treasure

Jesus looked at him and loved him. "One thing you lack," he said.
"Go, sell everything you have and give to the poor,
and you will have treasure in heaven. Then come, follow me."

MARK 10:21 NIV

The treasure we want is ours, already here, waiting. Jesus said so. He loved the rich young man who asked the secret to eternal life. He loves us when we ask. And the answer is the same. Whether it's wealth or power or ego or whatever else stands between us and God, an *abundance of treasure* is just on the other side. It's when we follow our Savior instead of our obsession, when we live for Him and not for something we've made or become, that we find the life we want, here and hereafter.

When we elevate the treasure we hold now above the one the Lord promises, we're following our own reasoning, the world's reasoning that has infected our hearts. It's the lie that says we can live our lives "halfway" for God. But He is not a halfway God. He holds nothing back from us—isn't it fair that He expects the same devotion? Then He blesses us more, because the *abundance of treasure* that follows isn't fair—we always receive far more than we give. He doesn't seem to mind.

What stands today between you and God? Will you follow the young man's example and go away "sad" (Mark 10:22 NIV), or will you follow your Savior and unleash the *abundance of treasure* He provides? This week is a great time to choose, don't you think?

Week 27
An Abundance of Rescue

"For the Son of Man came to seek and to save what was lost."

LUKE 19:10 NIV

I love the story of Zacchaeus. He climbed a sycamore tree in Jericho to catch a glimpse of Jesus and wound up entertaining the Lord. How descriptive of his faith! Zacchaeus, too, was wealthy, but unlike the young ruler who chose to ignore Jesus' teaching, he chose to make amends for his mistakes. He gave to the poor and repaid four times over anyone he had cheated. The Lord provided him with an *abundance of rescue* when he made the choice to follow Him. He does the same for us.

The Lord rescued dishonest tax collectors, the sick, and the lonely two thousand years ago, and He rescues us today. Our lost state is temporary because His grace is eternal. God is seeking you today, eager to join you in your home and rescue you from whatever threatens your peace. Zacchaeus found peace when he did what he knew to do, when he trusted in a God greater than all his wealth. Don't you want that same peace, that same excitement that would make you climb a tree in joy? You can have it when you prepare to be rescued from your past.

Let the Lord work His *abundance of rescue* on you this week. Feel Him leading you and saving you from anything in your life that hurts. Invite Him into your home and heart and be blessed by your relationship with the living God.

Week 28
An Abundance of Faith

Then the woman, knowing what had happened to her,
came and fell at his feet and,
trembling with fear, told him the whole truth. He said to her,
"Daughter, your faith has healed you.
Go in peace and be freed from your suffering."

MARK 5:33–34 NIV

We, too, are often "trembling with fear" about so many things. The woman Jesus spoke about was afraid, singled out in front of strangers, and yet she found the courage to tell "the whole truth," to put her faith in a Lord who would not forsake or deny her. That's an *abundance of faith* we want for ourselves, isn't it?

What do you do that causes you to tremble with fear? Do you ever feel like your faith is on display, out there for everyone to see? I think I feel that way, fearful and exposed, in my work sometimes. The task is always bigger than I think it's going to be, and I begin to doubt and question my fitness for it. But I need only reach out and touch Him and my faith is real again. I can do what I know and go in peace, never denying my Lord but finding the courage to follow Him with an *abundance of faith* that can sustain all my fears.

How's your faith right now? Have you been afraid to reach out to God, to follow your heart? Even when you tremble, you are strong. Reacquaint yourself with your *abundance of faith* this week and see the steadying power in store for you.

Week 29
An Abundance of Change

And he said: "I tell you the truth,
unless you change and become like little children,
you will never enter the kingdom of heaven."

MATTHEW 18:3 NIV

One amazing trait of little children is their ability, even desire, to forgive, adapt, and make the best of all that happens, eager to believe in those who love them. Even grown up now, we're all weak and afraid sometimes, struggling to find our way, sometimes becoming bitter or lost to a life that hurts us. But we can change, Jesus says. We can forgive, adapt, and make the best of all that happens. We can believe with the belief of a child, trust with our hearts in the Lord's grace, and begin today to simplify our relationship with Him. We can become His child again, ready to learn and be led, ready to give up our stubborn and resistant ways. It's an *abundance of change* we can take hold of at any moment.

Jesus has a special place in His heart for little ones, and He told His followers so more than once. We are *all* His "little ones." He waits eagerly for us to come to Him, to find sanctuary in His arms, to trust with our whole hearts. We grow and learn, but we never outgrow our need for our Lord. The more we embrace that need, the closer we get to Him. Our *abundance of change* lets us embrace it through everything in our lives. Our Lord will never turn away one of His children.

Are you on a path you want, or is there room for

change? How can you become more like the little children Jesus talked about? Don't be afraid to trust again. Your *abundance of change* never expires, and each day gives you the chance to exercise it, making more of your relationship with your Lord. It's more of Him, less of everything else that works best. What will you change this week?

Week 30
An Abundance of Creativity

The blessing of the LORD makes one rich,
and He adds no sorrow with it.

PROVERBS 10:22 NKJV

When my cousins and I were kids, we'd rake pine straw into rooms and make houses in the dirt. We'd swipe lawn chairs and five-gallon buckets for furniture and serve ourselves rocks on leaves. It was a game of riches to us, full of scavenged bounty fueled by fertile imaginations.

There was no real point to the straw rooms, but I remember how much fun it was to devote entire summer days to them. It was an *abundance of creativity* we shared, and though the straw was always the same, the game was always different. It never failed to provide new joys. We could do anything in our straw world because the only boundaries were ones we created on our own.

I doubt young girls rake pine straw into houses today, but if not, they don't know what they're missing. How about you? Do you take the time to notice the Lord's blessings of creativity in your life? Have you forgotten the joy of raking your piles of straw anywhere you want? Let your mind play and create a new world. An *abundance of creativity* waits for you to put it to use.

Week 31
An Abundance of Testimony

*Many of the Samaritans from that town believed in him
because of the woman's testimony,
"He told me everything I ever did."*

JOHN 4:39 NIV

Despite her past and her present, Jesus spent time in the presence of the woman drawing water from a well in Sychar. He told her who He was and redeemed her with omnipotent grace, when the "proper" women of the town wouldn't even go to the well at the same time she did. And when she left the Savior, she couldn't keep quiet about Him. She was possessed by an *abundance of testimony* that served to lead others to Him, as well.

We all have the same testimony to share if we'll dare. We may have to risk ridicule or disbelief, and we may find ourselves defending our right to know such wonders and to claim such a Savior for ourselves. But when He speaks to us and spends time with us, it's just not possible to keep the blessings to ourselves.

Think about your *abundance of testimony* this week. Will you share something about God's grace, or maybe His patience or His wisdom? You don't have to build a pulpit or stand on a street corner to tell your story. A few truthful words of gratitude for your Father are a testimony. A brief touch of compassion or unexpected forgiveness is a testimony. You can live your *life* as a testimony because God has abundantly blessed it.

Week 32
An Abundance of Optimism

A righteous man may have many troubles,
but the LORD delivers him from them all.

PSALM 34:19 NIV

We can all usually benefit from a little more optimism in our lives, especially when the trials of this world bear down on us and we feel overwhelmed by so much out of our control. It's much easier sometimes to give in to the pessimism of a broken heart, but it's the *abundance of optimism* from the Lord we need to hold on to instead.

Optimism from the Lord isn't a blind, head-in-the-sand hope that things will turn out all right. It's a conviction, a trust, a habit, and it affects the way we look at our world. We don't have to deny our troubles or even expect to solve them all right away, but we can open ourselves up to the Lord's delivery from what ails us. It may come in the form of a problem solved, or it may be a deeper understanding of a trouble we've struggled with for years; but we can always await its coming with eagerness. We prepare for the Lord's delivery by claiming our optimism in spite of any complication or test. He will not forsake us.

As you study your troubles this week, look at them with an *abundance of optimism* and trust that God has already prepared your delivery from them. His ways are many and varied, and you may have to wait awhile to see how He delivers you each time—but He will. You can count on that, and you can hold on to your optimism no matter what.

Week 33
An Abundance of Persistence

Then Jesus answered,
"Woman, you have great faith! Your request is granted."
And her daughter was healed from that very hour.

MATTHEW 15:28 NIV

The Gentile woman with the sick daughter knew Jesus had the power to heal her. She cried out to Him, and He didn't respond to her at first, possibly to judge her faith. Finally, He answered her and healed her daughter with one breath. The woman refused to give up when she knew she was right about Jesus' power and grace. Her *abundance of persistence* saved her daughter's life. How strong is yours?

Can you remember a time when you refused to give up? Perhaps others called you stubborn or pushy. I've heard those words a few times myself. We have to be careful about our persistence, taking the time to learn if we should continue in a direction about a job or a relationship, for example. But there's never any doubt when it comes to our faith. When we cry out, the Lord will respond and we will be blessed. If we abandon our *abundance of persistence*, we'll never know what wonders the Lord holds for us.

God can handle your relentless pursuit of Him, so exercise your *abundance of persistence* to the fullest this week. Go to God with all your questions and listen intently for His answers. Ask for wisdom and direction with the expectation of receiving it. He will not turn you away. When your faith guides your persistence, the result is an audience with God. Enjoy.

Week 34
An Abundance of Touch

He tends his flock like a shepherd:
He gathers the lambs in his arms
and carries them close to his heart.

ISAIAH 40:11 NIV

People often laugh a little when they see me garden. I've tried otherwise, but the only way I can tend to the tiny seedlings or sprawling plants is sitting on my backside. I make my way from plant to plant with only a pair of gloves and my one tool, what my husband calls a "baby hoe." It fits in my pocket.

When I try to stand upright and use a regular hoe, I destroy more than the weeds because I'm just too far away from my work. So I sit on the ground where I can put my hands on each plant and grip each weed. The Lord is a little like that, gardening me with an *abundance of touch*. He bends down to my level and puts His healing hand exactly where it's needed. He's not far away, stabbing at my heart the way I do with a long-handled hoe. He's close enough to touch my heart with His.

The Lord's *abundance of touch* is personal, pervasive, persistent. He won't let go just because we squirm or need more weeding. He's not afraid to sweat and toil for our growth. Do you know His *abundance of touch*? Do you feel Him close and quiet, connecting with you where you are? Take notice each time you feel God reach out to you this week. Let His touch heal you and guide you and comfort you. You are His garden.

Week 35
An Abundance of Opportunity

*"The God who made the world and everything in it
is the Lord of heaven and earth
and does not live in temples built by hands."*

ACTS 17:24 NIV

Okay, then where does He live? Where will we find Him? How will we hear Him? He makes it easy for us. *He lives where we are.* God listens to our cries and responds. He is not constrained by walls or borders, by fears or ignorance. Perhaps He's come to you in your car or your office. Maybe you've felt Him in a neighbor's kindness or a child's trust. Or maybe you've found Him living in the most unlikely place—at the depth of your fallenness, when you've run away and tried to hide. Was He there? Was there no temple around, and yet the presence of the almighty God filled your heart? That's because He provides an *abundance of opportunity* to open the door of your heart, because *that* is where He chooses to dwell.

If we pay attention to the *abundance of opportunity* in our lives, we'll be amazed. I've heard the Lord in my kitchen, argued with Him on my walks, discussed the future with Him in my garden. I've been surprised to look around and realize He didn't abandon me when I was unfaithful to Him. As long as there is the tiniest opening in my heart, the slightest breath that believes, there is opportunity for Him to enter. And He'll take it. He'll turn everything into an affirmation of His love and grace. The abundance never ends.

When did you last recognize the *abundance of opportunity* God prepared for you? Can you think of a time you overlooked it? What happened when you opened your heart to Him in an unlikely place? Pay attention this week and don't miss a single opportunity to find the Lord where He lives.

Week 36
An Abundance of Humanness

Immediately the boy's father exclaimed,
"I do believe; help me overcome my unbelief!"

MARK 9:24 NIV

Jesus healed the man's son when the man asked, reminding him that all things are possible when we believe. And yet we are often like the man in the story—believing as best we can and still knowing there is a level we haven't attained. The man's cry was not an excuse but a petition—"Help me deal with this part of my human, flawed, and finite self as I work to become more like You, closer to You." It's the same *abundance of humanness* we all share, the struggle our Lord understands.

We all suffer from the human emotions of doubt and fear sometimes, but because God is *more than human*, He can use our weaknesses to show us His strength. Often we feel closest to our Lord in times of trial and pain, when we're too afraid to do anything but pray. What a great idea! When we abandon our human tendencies to worry or doubt, God scoops them up and settles something else in their place, a little more of Him. Maybe you'll find a passage of scripture you'll claim just for yourself. Maybe a friend will appear just when you need her. Maybe you'll forgive a hurt so you can receive a blessing. We'll always fall prey to our humanness, but we can always rely on the superhuman touch of God's Spirit to correct what we've corrupted.

Do you normally complain about your *abundance of*

humanness, your failures, and your imperfections? Instead, turn your complaint or excuse into a petition for the Lord's touch this week. Unmask your greatest failing and ask Him to help you "overcome" whatever is troubling you. Just like in the story, He will respond.

Week 37
An Abundance of Assurance

Look, there on the mountains,
the feet of one who brings good news, who proclaims peace!
Celebrate your festivals, O Judah, and fulfill your vows.
No more will the wicked invade you;
they will be completely destroyed.

NAHUM 1:15 NIV

Nahum, a prophet at the time the Assyrians ruled over Judah, wrote to the oppressed Israelites to assure them of God's control. We need the same *abundance of assurance* in our lives today, when we feel defeated and captive. We sometimes have to be reminded in days of pain and confusion to hold on to our trust in God's plan for our lives, but we need never doubt. He is still here. We can still celebrate our festivals and fulfill our vows—we can still worship and work the ways we know how.

Our circumstances don't have to dictate our degree of devotion. We have a Savior who is always at work in this world, even when we don't see or understand His timing or methods. Still, we can trust that the same assurance the people of Judah were given belongs to us. Our invasions of the wicked will pass, too.

If you've let a difficult situation discourage or defeat you, claim your *abundance of assurance* this week. The Lord has not broken a promise yet, and He won't start now. Celebrate, fulfill, and rest assured in God's control.

Week 38
An Abundance of Camaraderie

A friend loves at all times,
and a brother is born for adversity.

Proverbs 17:17 NIV

We have a very strange dog and a stranger cat. Our dog, a lanky husky, still plays with the cat the way he did as a pup, and the forever patient tabby tolerates it. Our dog is harmless and good-natured to everything except nonhuman intruders in his space. Those mammals, particularly cats, are in danger because he attacks even in a fenced yard before we can intervene.

We find it strange enough that he loves our cat while making it his goal to rid the world of all others. The stranger part is how our cat behaves during these seek-and-destroy missions. He gets himself a front-row seat and watches with a feline's uncharacteristic concentration. The two have a total disdain for every other four-legged or feathered creature that comes around, but they support each other through the strangest thick and thin. They're a crazy pair, but they demonstrate the *abundance of camaraderie* we all want to enjoy.

We all want someone who will stand by us, be on our side in a dispute, and support us when we're doing all we know to do. When we feel that camaraderie from another, we find strength and courage to carry on. And when we offer the same to a friend, we receive a blessing ourselves.

Have you enjoyed the *abundance of camaraderie* God

created for you lately? He wants us to be there for each other, to be unafraid to show our support and enjoy each other's victories. See how much camaraderie you can enjoy this week.

Week 39
An Abundance of Resistance

Be self-controlled and alert.
Your enemy the devil prowls around like
a roaring lion looking for someone to devour.
Resist him, standing firm in the faith,
because you know that your brothers throughout the world
are undergoing the same kind of sufferings.

1 PETER 5:8–9 NIV

The Christians in Peter's time faced all kinds of torment. Today we face the torment of a world where tangible trappings may lure us away from our goals—and resisting is exhausting. Maybe that's why we give in to the temptations around us more easily than we'd like. Daily we fight things that tempt us away from the great life God has planned, and sometimes we lose, giving in to doubt or laziness or impurity or selfishness or irresponsibility. But our *abundance of resistance* remains because it lives in our hearts.

We can resist whatever we want when we *stop* fighting. That tiring tug-of-war we allow ourselves to have is the justifying and bargaining and conniving that hides our faith. If, instead, we uncover the faith in our hearts and put that up against the temptation, we'll see quickly which one is stronger. We let our faith in God fight the fight so we don't have to.

Have you needed to claim your *abundance of resistance* lately? Have you exhausted yourself fighting a fight you didn't have to enter? When you're faced with a temptation this week, let your faith do the fighting for you. Resisting doesn't have to be so hard.

Week 40
An Abundance of Gathering

"He who is not with me is against me,
and he who does not gather with me scatters."

MATTHEW 12:30 NIV

We are daily witnesses, and everything counts. What a wonderful gift! We don't have to be leaders of nations or even members of the PTA to do something great every day for God, to gather instead of scatter. When you reach out to someone in need, with just a note or a kind word, that counts. When you forgive someone who hurt you instead of retaliating, that counts. When you extend empathy and understanding in a difficult situation, that counts. Every action is one that gathers to God's kingdom or scatters those who need Him away. We never know what impact our simple actions will have, but we can be sure they matter somewhere.

When readers write to me, they probably don't have any idea what they do for me. They gather me into the crucible of their faith, they tell me about their victories, and they witness with the simple action of a letter. They freely use their *abundance of gathering*, and it counts more than they know.

How have you been blessed with others' *abundance of gathering*? I know you can remember many examples. And how have you used your own? It doesn't have to be a big, extravagant event. The smallest actions speak loudly. Try it this week.

Week 41
An Abundance of Cleanliness

"What goes into a man's mouth does not make him 'unclean,' but what comes out of his mouth, that is what makes him 'unclean.'"

MATTHEW 15:11 NIV

No one has ever accused me of being a good housekeeper and likely never will. That's okay, because the charge for cleanliness here has nothing to do with those skills. My thoughts and words and actions are what threaten me where it matters, not my unmopped floors (though they could stand some help, too). The Lord guides us all to an *abundance of cleanliness* if we choose to follow Him. Only He can clean what we've perverted.

Just as we pick the foods we eat and how we prepare them, we pick the life we lead and how we live it. It's our responsibility how clean or unclean that is. And it's our pain we have to deal with when we've pushed away from God instead of toward Him. I know you know some of those choices well, the choice for anything contrary to God's nature. Every time we opt for more anger or hate or destruction, we make a mess. But all is not lost, because the Lord knows what to do with it and how to teach us better.

Notice your thoughts and words this week. Are they of damaging things that can harm you or others? Or are they thoughts and words of peace and solution and grace? Claim your *abundance of cleanliness* by letting the Lord purge your heart of "evil thoughts" (Matthew 15:19NIV) and restore you in His will. Every thought of Him is one less thought of something that hurts.

Week 42
An Abundance of Discretion

See to it that no one takes you captive through hollow
and deceptive philosophy, which depends on human tradition
and the basic principles of this world rather than on Christ.

COLOSSIANS 2:8 NIV

It's a long drive on I-40 to the Grand Canyon, so on our trip, my husband and I ate a lot. We carried a box of snacks and found new goodies along the way, sharing most. I opened a single-serve applesauce. "Want a bite?" I asked as I dug in with a plastic spoon. "Is it cold?" my husband asked and then immediately opened his mouth. "No," I said and plopped the loaded spoon inside.

I've never seen that look on anybody's face before. Roadkill on that spoon couldn't have made it worse. He was trying to swallow while his eyes looked crazy at me like I'd tried to poison him, disbelieving the predicament he was in and my overpowering laughter I couldn't contain. I could barely see through teary eyes, and my stomach hurt the rest of the day. It took him forever to get his breath.

"What'd you give me that for?" he finally blurted out.

"You opened your mouth" was my only defense. Apparently cold applesauce would have been okay, but warm was definitely not. Sometimes we don't wait for the answers we need and ignore the *abundance of discretion* our Lord has given us. Things far more serious than a bad bite of applesauce hurt us because we fail to reason, because we let someone lead us the wrong way, or because we just don't pay attention to the lessons the Lord is trying to teach us.

Maybe you've found yourself in a predicament you

could have avoided if you'd used a little more discretion. Maybe you're facing a decision right now—have you gathered all your facts? There is nothing you can't figure out, and God is waiting to help you each step of the way. Talk to Him this week, listen for His leanings, and get the answers you need before you act. Tap into the *abundance of discretion* He has given you.

Week 43
An Abundance of Overcoming

"Those whom I love I rebuke and discipline.
So be earnest, and repent. Here I am!
I stand at the door and knock.
If anyone hears my voice and opens the door,
I will come in and eat with him, and he with me.
To him who overcomes,
I will give the right to sit with me on my throne."

REVELATION 3:19–21 NIV

We sometimes fight the Lord's discipline, don't we? We don't like to acknowledge our failures and admit how far we've strayed from His will. But God continues to pursue us, even when we've run away with all our disobedience. He stands ready to restore us to His kingdom when we'll let Him into our hearts. He makes the way for our *abundance of overcoming*, standing there with saving grace to make us whole again.

The choice to turn away from Him was ours, and the choice to overcome all the messes we've made is ours. God knows we'll make the first choice because we're human and flawed, but He waits to see if we'll make the second choice. Will we accept His discipline for the love and instruction it is, or will we ignore His voice and leave the door on an eternal life closed?

Have you recognized the *abundance of overcoming* God has given you? Have you realized the depth of His love and forgiveness and determination to save you, how He eagerly wants to gather you to Him when you want the same? Touch it this week. The past can be overcome with the Lord's abundance of grace.

Week 44
An Abundance of Competence

Such confidence as this is ours through Christ before God.
Not that we are competent in ourselves to claim
anything for ourselves, but our competence comes from God.
He has made us competent as ministers of a new covenant—
not of the letter but of the Spirit;
for the letter kills, but the Spirit gives life.

2 CORINTHIANS 3:4–6 NIV

We'll never be perfect, but God knows that already. And no matter how hard we try to obey in every situation, our human side will win sometimes and we'll fail the letter of the law. But God's instruction to us is more than a doctrine we could memorize. Living in His Spirit is our goal—a life of commitment to Him even though we'll fall and are unworthy of His bountiful grace.

Despite our need for His constant guidance, or maybe because of it, He entrusts us with His covenant and delivers to us an *abundance of competence* to live it the best we can and share it with others. No, we're not perfect, but our lack of perfection doesn't make our ministry go away. Forever connected to His Spirit, we can go to others, competent to witness of His love and grace and, if He wills, be a guide to lead them to Him, too.

When we feel incompetent, we have two choices. We can stay that way, or we can step out in faith, learn what the Lord intended, and find joy in our work. Don't be afraid. This week reconnect your spirit to God's and let Him guide you in a new step of your ministry. You have the *abundance of competence* He gives us all.

Week 45
An Abundance of Self-Reliance

But let each one examine his own work,
and then he will have rejoicing in
himself alone, and not in another.
For each one shall bear his own load.

GALATIANS 6:4–5 NKJV

I know 412 wrong ways to hang a window shade. You might not consider that something to be proud of, but I do. (I'm easily entertained.) I know hanging shades is a little thing anybody can do, but the task was a real challenge for me. I could have asked someone else to do it, but like a toddler with a spoon too big, I wanted to do it myself.

So I struggled, grunted, threatened the person who wrote the instructions, fell off the ladder, and ruined the saw I took from my husband's shop (don't ask). But today I have shades everywhere. And the victory was worth all the defeats. Yes, shades are a little conquest, but they're *my* little conquest. Next time maybe I'll move up to blinds. . . .

We learn so much when we determine to do things for ourselves, even if it's just covering the windows. God puts lessons in every goofy thing we do, no matter how long it takes us to do it (the seasons changed before I finished my project). And while window treatments aren't exactly spiritual high points, they're part of the everyday world where we live and breathe. Our victories are important wherever we find them. God will guide us to an *abundance of self-reliance* in shades today and something far more important or fun tomorrow.

Having new challenges to tackle is a wonderful part of life. Where have you found your self-reliance lately? Where is it lacking? Choose one small project this week, set a date, and prepare to enjoy the *abundance of self-reliance* that finds you.

Week 46
An Abundance of Harvest

But when He saw the multitudes,
He was moved with compassion for them,
because they were weary and scattered,
like sheep having no shepherd.
Then He said to His disciples,
"The harvest truly is plentiful,
but the laborers are few."

MATTHEW 9:36–37 NKJV

It can be easy to feel overwhelmed and saddened by all the suffering in this world. There is pain and hunger and violence and lostness everywhere. The same was true when Jesus walked the earth. The "weary and scattered" sheep needed guidance and care then, and those among us need it now. No matter where we are, the *abundance of harvest* awaits. What can we do?

There will always be more pain than we can ease by ourselves, but we can start. Every act of kindness or generosity to one person can touch someone else. Every bit of respect and honor you teach your children can reach those they touch. Every way you live your life for God can serve as an example for those you know and those you don't. Everything you give to one will be a testament to the rest. We don't have to rescue the whole lost herd, but we can start with one.

Have you thought about your *abundance of harvest* lately? Do you pay attention to the small opportunities to give, because they're important to all if they're important to one? How will you minister to a weary and scattered one this week?

Week 47
An Abundance of Dependence

"In his hand is the life of every creature and the breath of all mankind."

JOB 12:10 NIV

We don't like to be dependent on anything or anyone, do we? We can't wait to be independent of our parents, and we resist dependence on friends or neighbors for help. Many of us fight dependencies on food or relationships or medication or television or some other trap. Being needy is a drain on our bodies and minds. But the *abundance of dependence* on our Lord is different.

When we depend on Him, we find great strength. When our every need is met, we never feel needy. When we depend on God's guidance and wisdom, we can live independent of the influences of this world that would misguide us. Our dependence on God will never be misplaced or refused. He is like a storm shelter in a tornado. When we depend on Him to save us, we live our lives encapsulated by His presence. Nothing can get into our hearts that He won't allow when we depend on Him to hold us.

Rediscover and enjoy your *abundance of dependence* this week, resting in God's powerful arms, knowing you are safe. He will answer your cries and guide your steps when you trust in Him. You can depend on His unquestionable faithfulness.

Week 48
An Abundance of Impatience

But I trust in you, O LORD;
I say, "You are my God." My times are in your hands.

PSALM 31:14–15 NIV

I know the Lord granted me an extra helping of this abundance! With the patience of a premature baby, I've hurried along every day of my life, trying to get God to line up my world the way I planned, already, *now*! He said no, many, many times. And He showed me how my *abundance of impatience* wasn't the curse I thought it was, but a blessing instead.

We can fight the Lord's timing, or we can rest in it. Every time we have to stop and wait, we can complain or we can commune with our God. He uses these times of inaction to work in our hearts, to speak to us when we won't stand still any other way. It may take us a long time to learn that the tangible things we wait on are never what the delay is about. Waiting isn't about what happens outside us—it's about what happens inside us. So we can wait with purpose as we wait with God.

Are you impatient for something now? It will happen, or it won't; but what will matter even more will be where you are when the wait is over. Will you have used your waiting time wisely, learning from the Lord instead of cursing the clock? Use your *abundance of impatience* while your hands and feet are stopped to move your heart and soul closer to the Lord. Work while you wait.

Week 49
An Abundance
of Encouragement

We have different gifts, according to the grace given us.
If it is encouraging, let him encourage.

ROMANS 12:6, 8 NIV

We get discouraged easily when the battle is hard or the road is long. Our fears and weaknesses envelop us like darkness, and our work suffers. Then we're blessed with an encouraging word, with a story of triumph, with a touch from our God. He provides an *abundance of encouragement* when we need it most.

Two wonderful friends have poured their *abundance of encouragement* on me as I've written this book. They have prayed for me, kept their faith in me, and never doubted me. They live far away, and their encouragement comes through cyberspace and fiber optics, but it's as real as a touch. And I am grateful.

I want to pass on that encouragement to others, and I know you do, too. Do you need to feel God's *abundance of encouragement* from others this week? Or are you in a position to share it with another? Either way, the blessings will overflow for giver and recipient. God will send you the encouragement you need and put those in your path who need it from you. Watch, share, receive, and enjoy.

Week 50
An Abundance of Hope

May the God of hope fill you with all joy and peace
as you trust in him,
so that you may overflow with hope
by the power of the Holy Spirit.

ROMANS 15:13 NIV

Do you feel the hope of God in your heart? That's a lot to ask when we're facing a life of challenge, doubt, and fear, isn't it? But what about the Lord's part of the deal? If He is the "God of hope," then don't you think He hopes in us, too? That's probably a lot to ask of Him, considering what a challenge we present sometimes. Yet He never considers us a lost cause, because He is filled with an *abundance of hope* for us all. He never shuts the door or refuses to answer when we knock. And we can do the same when we claim our *abundance of hope* in Him.

Surely if God sees possibility in us, regardless of the messes we manage to get ourselves in, we can follow His lead. If we can hope because God does, then we can hope in the power He has to rescue us and in the commitment He made to restore us. That kind of hope is coupled with the trust that we can't fall outside God's grace, and it sustains us the same way it sustains God.

Are you filled with hope this week? Touch the power of your *abundance of hope* so you can touch the possibility of all your life can become. Hope begins the process, and then it allows the work to make it a reality. Hope in God because He hopes in you.

Week 51
An Abundance of Joy

Though the fig tree does not bud and there are no grapes on the vines,
though the olive crop fails and the fields produce no food,
though there are no sheep in the pen and no cattle in the stalls,
yet I will rejoice in the LORD, I will be joyful in God my Savior.

HABAKKUK 3:17–18 NIV

Finding happiness in a heartbreak is tough. Smiling through the pain seems impossible. We want our lives to be full of joy and peace all the time. And they can be. No, I haven't discovered the secret to perfection, only a reliance on God's control. If we believe He holds us in the palm of His hand even when our "crops" fail, we can rest in the joy of a life in His charge. We don't have to see the bounty to trust it's coming when we need it.

A life walked with God provides us with an *abundance of joy* regardless of the circumstances we face. I know how hard that is to believe, but it's true. And it can seem harder to live when you're hurting and lost and facing so many troubles. Where is the joy then? It's in your relationship with your Lord, in what comes first, just like I've talked about throughout this book.

When you have *more of God* in your heart, there is *more joy*, no matter what happens in the world. It isn't the fleeting happiness of an unexpected promotion or a good haircut that makes your life worth living, but the powerful and pervasive joy of living your purpose and reaching your goals under God's control, even in the midst of temporary crop failures.

Have you equated your *abundance of joy* with passing conditions of a tangible world? Or do you see that your joy is ensured when your heart belongs to God? Live in your *abundance of joy* this week, as if you've just discovered it, and you'll never want to let it go again.

Week 52
An Abundance of Peace

And let the peace of God rule in your hearts,
to which also you were called in one body; and be thankful.

COLOSSIANS 3:15 NKJV

Peace and gratitude are linked, always, because gratitude displaces any kind of unrest. And it's our choice. Paul told the believers in Colosse that it was their choice to let the peace of God rule, and we hear him now. If we don't feel God's peace in our hearts, surely it's a problem with the receiver, not the Giver.

When we couch all our prayers in gratitude, we create a willing heart. We remind ourselves of God's love and call Him ever nearer—knowing He will not refuse us. We recognize that the God who is capable of providing all we need gives His *abundance of peace* with every gift.

God's peace comes with His forgiveness, His compassion, His direction, His simplicity, order, and insight, too—because everything He does is about instilling more peace in our hearts. It's up to us to accept. Will you let God's peace rule in your heart today and every day? Thank Him for giving you that choice. Make the same choice every day, and it'll give you a different world. The problems of a human life will remain, but you will face them differently. When you start there, with gratitude for His presence, His *abundance of peace* rules. Start today.

· · · · ·

Contact the Author:

Karon Goodman
P.O. Box 3226
Oxford, Alabama 36203

NOTES

NOTES

NOTES

NOTES

NOTES

NOTES

If you enjoyed

ANOTHER FINE MESS, LORD!

be sure to read these other titles by

KARON PHILLIPS GOODMAN

Grab a Broom, Lord—
There's Dust Everywhere!

*The Imperfect Woman's Guide
to God's Grace*

ISBN 1-58660-918-1

God's grace is more powerful than life's
imperfections, as you'll discover in this
delightfully wise guide to living a full,
powerful life in the security of God's grace.

You Still Here, Lord?

*The Insecure Woman's Guide
to God's Faithfulness*

ISBN 1-59310-137-6

Insecurity is no match for God's faithfulness! This timely guide shows readers how
to live securely in the knowledge of God's
character, commitment, and care.

You're Late Again, Lord!

The Impatient Woman's Guide to God's Timing

ISBN 1-58660-410-4

Witty writing and thoughtful insights
for any woman who's questioned God's
timing, with encouragement to spend
waiting time purposefully.